WEI KUEN DO

HISTORY & PRACTICE

WEI KUEN DO: HISTORY AND PRACTICE
Copyright © 2017 by Ti Tzu
—First Edition—
ISBN-10: 0692589260
ISBN-13: 978-0692589267

All rights reserved. No part of this book may be reproduced in any form without prior, written permission from the publisher or author, except in the case of brief quotations in articles or reviews.

The material in this book is intended for educational purposes only. No one should undertake the practice of self-defense or healing without qualified instruction and supervision, and an awareness of the criminal and civil limitations on the use of force in self-defense and the practice of medicine. Physical combat is an inherently dangerous activity. Medical diagnosis and treatment should be provided by qualified healthcare professionals. The author, publisher and distributors are not responsible in any manner for any injury or liability that may result from practicing—or attempting to practice—the techniques described herein. Any application of the information contained herein is at the reader's sole and exclusive risk. As a result of the risk of injury to oneself and others, prior to engaging in any type of self-defense program it is advisable to consult both a professional martial arts instructor and a licensed physician.

This book was printed in the United States of America by Stirling Bridge Publications; a publisher specializing in works dedicated to exploring the power of one.

stirlingbridge@mail.com

滙拳道

This work is dedicated to
Wei Kuen Do
Founder and Headmaster

Leo T. Fong

For kindnesses too numerous to count;
treasures too precious to value;
and wisdom too profound to measure.

CONTENTS

	Foreword	1
I	Introduction	4
II	Guideposts	9
III	The Ultimate is Within You	14
IV	Genesis of a Warrior-Priest	17
V	Western Boxing	20
VI	Judo, Wrestling, Tang Soo Do, Jujitsu	28
VII	Choy Lay Fut Kung Fu	31
VIII	Sil Lum Kung Fu	35
IX	Arnis/Escrima	39
X	Jeet Kune Do	45
XI	The Lee-Fong Connection	47
XII	The Way of the Integrated Fist	54
XIII	Always Striving, Never Arriving…	57
XIV	The Tools	61
XV	The Angles of Attack	70
XVI	The Circles of Destruction	86
XVII	The Trapping Combinations	118
XVIII	Develop, Refine, Dissolve, Express	129
IXX	Acronym, Analogy, Alliteration	131
XX	Friends, Family, Followers	137
XXI	The Words of the Grandmaster	174

滙拳道

FOREWORD

WEI KUEN DO: YESTERDAY, TODAY AND TOMORROW
BY THOMAS J. NARDI, PH. D.

My first introduction to Leo Fong was through books and magazine articles in the 1960s when I had just begun my martial arts studies. When I first heard of him, little did I imagine how our paths would one day cross and join. He was on the cover of the November 1970 issue of *Black Belt* magazine and the May 1971 issue of *Karate Illustrated*. In the *Black Belt* article, Leo exposed the weaknesses of the major fighting styles. His keen analytical approach to combat was clear in this article, and one can see that he was quite an innovator at that time. He was also well versed in the traditional Chinese arts, having studied with many legendary Chinese masters. In *Karate Illustrated* Leo presented the tiger claw techniques of Sil Lum Kung Fu. He had several books published by Ohara publications including one on another traditional Chinese art: Choy Lay Fut Kung Fu. Ohara also published Leo's book on weight training. This book, co-authored with Ron Marchini, was probably the first to advocate a scientific approach to martial arts by utilizing supplemental weight training.

Leo's desire to share information and help others on their martial arts journeys led him to form Koinonia Productions. The name of the company immediately caught my eye. I recognized the word "koinonia" from my own studies of New Testament Greek. Although difficult to translate exactly, it connotes a willingness to share for the greater good; working in fellowship for the benefit of the community. The term resonated with me: Here was someone who had a deep spiritual foundation as well as martial arts expertise.

Among the books published by Koinonia were the foundational text for Leo's art: <u>Wei Kuen Do, The Psychodynamic Art of Free Fighting</u>.

Psychodynamic? As a clinical psychologist, I was intrigued; as a martial artist with black belts in several martial arts, including Goju-ryu Karate and Japanese Jujutsu, I was impressed. Of course I had to have it! I purchased a copy, studied its contents and practiced the techniques diligently. Leo's strong foundation in Western Boxing—including Golden Gloves and collegiate competitions, as well as unsanctioned "smokers"—was clearly evident. Also evident was his deep understanding and application of other traditional martial arts.

I was fascinated by Leo's martial arts accomplishments and his professional achievements. I discovered that, in addition to his bachelor's degree in physical education, Leo had master's degrees in both theology and social work. I was very pleased to find someone with whom I could discuss the deeper spiritual and psychological aspects of the martial arts.

In 1980, Koinonia published my book: The Mind in the Martial Arts. It was the first of its kind to propose and advance the psychological aspects of the martial arts. My friendship with Leo continued to grow over the years as I eagerly absorbed Leo's philosophy and teachings of the physical, spiritual, mental and psychological aspects of Wei Kuen Do. Leo encouraged me to continue to write and Koinonia published several more of my books.

In 1993, Leo and I co-founded the Total Approach Organization ("TAO") to promote the advanced study of the totality of the martial arts, including the combative psycho-spiritual, and healing aspects. We have done countless seminars and training camps over the years, bringing Wei Kuen Do, Modern Escrima and the healing art of Chi Fung to hundreds of eager students.

Leo has been, and remains, my teacher, mentor, spiritual director, business partner, role model, and, most important of all, my friend. We have shared the Wei Kuen Do journey together for many decades. Wei Kuen Do was first conceived in 1974 in Hong Kong when Leo was encouraged to synthesize his many years of martial arts and combat sports experience into a dynamic art. He named his art: *Wei Kuen Do, the way of the assimilated or integrated fist.* Although conceived in 1974, Wei Kuen Do's "birthday" might be considered to be July 8, 2008; the date it was officially registered as a trademark by Leo and myself.

I have not sought the spotlight, but have remained in the background while helping to propagate Leo's teachings through the seminars we have conducted together, as well as in articles I have written. I have written about Leo and his art in many articles published in the United States and

Europe. I also produced a documentary, "The Arkansas Dragon," about his life and many accomplishments.

    I am very pleased that so many people are now practicing Wei Kuen Do. It makes me happy to see how many people are embracing Leo's techniques and philosophy. Their use of the name Wei Kuen Do, however, is always contingent upon their remaining in good standing; that is, meeting the standards determined by Leo and monitored by the both of us. Unfortunately some people are more accomplished with the techniques of Wei Kuen Do than with its philosophy. Embracing the deeper philosophical and spiritual dimensions is what sets Wei Kuen Do practitioners apart from other martial artists. Although there are many skilled practitioners of Wei Kuen Do, no one person will inherit this art—it belongs to all who truly follow its teachings, and the name "Wei Kuen Do" will remain trademarked property belonging to of Leo and me. Mastery of techniques alone does not equate with proficiency in Wei Kuen Do. The techniques are the body of Wei Kuen Do; its soul and spirit are found in its philosophy and spiritual dimension.

    In addition to being a clinical and sports psychologist, I am also the Director of Counseling Programs in School Counseling and Mental Health Counseling at Long Island University's Rockland and West Point campuses. In the graduate counseling courses I teach, I often quote Leo's words to my students: *"Some people do things to impress the impressionable."* Psychologically, some people have a need to impress others and some people have a needed to be easily impressed. Our society seems to thrive on exaggeration and hyperbole. Martial arts tournaments have special divisions for black belts under the age of five. There are twenty year old "grand masters." Exaggeration and deception, of others and/or oneself, are not the exclusive domain of martial artists. People take a one weekend class and are suddenly "experts" on the topic presented. Someone is an extra in a crowd scene in and then considers himself a movie star. Television presents "celebrities" who are celebrities because they are famous for being famous.

    Leo Fong stands out all the more because he is a true and legitimate master. His mastery is not restricted to the martial arts. His accomplishments in ministry, writing, film, social work, exercise science, combat arts and life itself speak for themselves. He needs no fluff or padding. He is an unique and iconic figure. I believe my life is richer because of him, as are the lives of all who follow his teachings.

I. INTRODUCTION
BY ADAM JAMES

While growing up in the New York City area and in Hawaii, I read Leo Fong's books on Kung Fu and Power Training, and saw his action movies. My father had been a U.S. Navy officer and I started training in the martial arts at a very young age. Also, my uncle was a boxing television producer and I grew up around boxing and wrestling.

I first met Leo Fong in 1994 at the Warner Center Club in the Los Angeles area, where I worked as a personal trainer and ran the martial arts program. Leo was a member of the club and we would often talk about martial arts, movies and life. Eventually we discussed making a television show entitled, "The Spirit of the Masters," and we began to work together. The concept of the show was for me to be the host and travel the world interviewing the greatest grandmasters of the martial arts. While we didn't make the show in the end, we started a friendship that has changed my life.

滙拳道

I began to train extensively with Leo in Wei Kuen Do, Leo's personal martial arts system. While he had written the book <u>Wei Kuen Do: the Psychodynamic Art of Free Fighting</u> in 1976, the style was mostly contained in his mind and heart. At the time, he had a clear concept of the art personally, and he could express it himself, but he had not yet developed a specific curriculum. Leo had numerous techniques and combinations in the original Wei Kuen Do book, and several other books like, <u>Strategies for Winning in Kung Fu and Karate</u> (published in 1977). However, it wasn't until we began training together that the exact curriculum began to take shape and the Wei Kuen Do combinations were created.

At first, Leo held boxing focus mitts for me, but he had a bad shoulder and holding the mitts aggravated it. So he began using soft Escrima sticks that were given to him by his friend, Sonny Umpad. The sticks were used like focus mitts as a target for striking. However, since the sticks were directed at a smaller target, the training evolved, because the fighter had to use greater aim and actually relax more. This provided the opportunity to emphasize the initial movement and focus on creating fluid combinations. Another benefit of the sticks was using them to strike at the fighter, thereby developing the defensive skills of slipping and parrying the attack. Over the years, we began to use PVC pipe wrapped in padding and duct tape, and we called them, "Focus Sticks."

Leo was inspired to create a series of combinations and he called these, "The Angles of Attack." They combined Kung Fu, Western Boxing, JKD and Escrima footwork. He called them "The Angles of Attack" because he recognized that the practitioner needed to hit and move so as to create angles or openings on the opponent, while at the same time changing and eliminating the angles that the opponent had on the practitioner.

Next, we worked on the defensive combinations called, "The Circles of Destruction." While the Angles of Attack could be trained for all situations, including defensive and counter attacks, the Circles of Destruction were specifically created to develop defensive skills.

Trapping is controversial in the martial arts community, and some people question if it would work in free fighting. "The Trapping Combinations" of Wei Kuen Do are made for free fighting, and they combine the trapping techniques of Wing Chun with a Western Boxing delivery system. Leo and I would practice extensively with the Focus Sticks and with free hands to perfect these combinations.

"The Quick Counters" came next. Leo always just calls them the Counters, but I like to call them "Quick Counters" to emphasize the quick and spontaneous delivery off the opponent's attack.

Eventually "The Faking Combinations," "New Expressions" and "Footwork Combinations" were developed. They all, however, have the same foundation as the Angles of Attack. In fact, you can see the key components of all the combinations in the original <u>Wei Kuen Do: The Psychodynamic Art of Free Fighting</u> book. The tools were always there; we just needed to polish, dissolve, and express them in a complete curriculum. Over the years, Leo and I worked to perfect the combinations and free fighting skills of Wei Kuen Do, and to release what was deep inside Leo from his early Western Boxing years and his training with Bruce Lee.

Also, during this time, Leo began to develop Chi Fung. He combined his knowledge of Tai Chi, Chi Gung, and weight training to create this new system of martial arts. Leo had started lifting weights as a boxer, and he used the methods of Barney Ross for inspiration and guidance. When he moved to Northern California, Leo began to train with "Mr. Universe," Bill Pearl, and Leo went on to co-write the pioneering book <u>Power Training for Karate and Kung Fu</u>. Leo was always an advocate of weight lifting and martial arts conditioning, and now he combined these principles and techniques. It's interesting to note that some Kung Fu instructors don't believe in weight lifting, and that some Western-based fighters don't believe in chi or energy training. However, Leo grasped both disciplines and he combined them to make a new and revolutionary approach to training.

Over the years, Leo and I also fine-tuned the system of Modern Escrima. Leo first began training in the Filipino martial arts while he was making films in the Philippines. When he arrived in Manila, Leo was recognized as a Kung Fu master but he always had an open mind to learning. He was introduced to Remy Presas, and Leo learned Modern Arnis from Remy. When Leo moved to Stockton, California, he met Angel Cabales, and Leo trained with Angel in his system of Serrada Escrima. Eventually, Leo combined Modern Arnis, Serrada Escrima, and Wei Kuen Do free fighting to create Modern Escrima.

Leo and I have had many adventures together and I have been honored to have him as my friend and teacher. When Leo was inducted into the Black Belt Magazine Hall of Fame, I wrote the inauguration article. Later *Black Belt* published an article I wrote detailing the friendship and mutual training development of Leo and Bruce Lee. Together, Leo and I have taught numerous seminars, with different and interesting concepts, like

汇拳道

"Irish Boxers for Saint Patrick's Day," "Beyond the Five Ways of Attack," "Movie Stunt Fighting, Modern Escrima and More." We have conducted a training session every weekend at the Warner Center Park for many years, and we have trained numerous top martial artists from around the world.

The friendship between Bruce and Leo had a big impact on both men. Leo has shared with me an inspirational moment that happened for him with Bruce, and this story had a huge impact on me as well. Leo and Bruce were together when Bruce asked Leo why he was running around town training in so many different styles. At the time, Leo was a black belt in Tae Kwon Do, Moo Duk Kwan and Judo/Jujitsu, and he was also training in Sil Lum Kung Fu, Choy Lay Fut Kung Fu, Wing Chun and Bruce's system of Jeet Kune Do. Leo replied that he was looking for the ultimate martial art. Bruce tapped Leo on the chest and said that the ultimate is inside of you. This touched Leo deeply because he recalled the passage in the Bible to the effect that that the Kingdom of God is within. Leo told me that the words resonated with him, not only in regard to martial arts, but also in life. He no longer looked outside for the secrets, but rather strove for self-development and self-awareness.

On September 11, 1992, a cross appeared in the window of Leo's home. His wife had a vision and felt the presence of God. Over the next few years, many people came to their house and helped to convert the room with the cross into a prayer room, and the living room into a chapel. Leo and his wife founded Holy Cross Canoga Park, and they have held a religious service there on the first Saturday of the month ever since. Leo told me one day that there are three reactions to seeing the cross. Some people examine the glass and look for a trick or an explanation. Others dismiss it and are not moved in any way. There are many, however, who have a deep spiritual awakening when they see the cross. It impacts them spiritually, regardless of their religion, and there have been some who claimed to have experienced healing or life changing results.

Leo has a special talent for giving a sermon. He told me once that while growing up in Arkansas, he didn't like the preachers who went on and on about religious doctrine and detailed bible quotes. One of Leo's teachers in the ministry taught him to tell a personal story and a joke, and then to connect it to the sermon's message. Also, he emphasized keeping it short and including a song, so that people are moved. His teacher told him that people are hungry and they need food for the soul.

In 2012, Leo and I made a pilot movie called "East of West," and it was a great learning experience for me. We wrote, directed, and produced the film together, and I played the lead role. Leo was incredible to work with and I learned so much from him as a filmmaker.

It's always amazing to me when I meet people who have known Leo over the years. He has been so many different things to different people. For some, he is the martial arts grandmaster who has inspired and taught them. For others, he is the movie star, and he has helped many people to get their start in the film industry. As a Methodist Minister, Leo has performed countless weddings and funerals; he has been a spiritual rock and guide for people during the most important moments in their lives.

For me, Leo has been my friend and teacher in martial arts, movies and ministry. I've been very blessed to have him in my life and he will always be a part of my heart, my mind and my soul.

滙拳道

II. GUIDEPOSTS

Leo Fong has been a practicing martial artist for nearly eight decades. ***Eight***. That's almost eighty years. The better part of a century. Somewhere in the neighborhood of three generations. Longer than most of us have been alive...

During this epic martial journey he has studied a wide variety of arts, both Western and Eastern, at the hands (and feet) of past masters. He absorbed what he found useful along the way and combined these teachings into an art called: *"Wei Kuen Do—The Way of the Integrated Fist."*

*****

Wei Kuen Do is a powerful, fluid and organic martial art, but it is more than a system of self-defense; it is also a way of life. And Grandmaster Fong is living proof of its effectiveness in every realm. He has purified his art in the crucible of combat, besting scores of opponents, winning many titles and receiving numerous accolades, including most recently his induction into the Modern Arnis Hall of Fame in June of 2014. And at eighty-seven years of age his workouts leave students literally a quarter his age gasping for breath.

He has written extensively in his field, having published dozens of titles on the martial arts and related subjects. He has starred in many films, both martial arts themed and otherwise, and he continues to write, direct, produce and appear on screen. And at the same time he has served the people of his community for decades as an ordained Methodist minister.

By any standard—combat effectiveness, physical fitness, recognized skill, adding to the recorded canon, promoting the art, or serving the community—Leo Fong is truly a grandmaster of the martial arts.

For many years, there was no official curriculum in Wei Kuen Do. But in 2012—the year of the dragon—that all changed. At a special gathering in California that autumn, Grandmaster Fong unveiled a consolidated syllabus of the fundamental forms of his system, and tested and certified a core group of his instructors from around the world in these methods, thereby establishing the shape of things to come.

GENESIS: THE 2012 SKY DRAGON FESTIVAL

This historic event was the genesis of the present work. In the wake of this special gathering, the idea was conceived to record the history and structure of Wei Kuen Do in book form, and to make it available to all who study this art in order provide a common base of knowledge and practice.

滙拳道

Many who read this book will already be familiar with Grandmaster Fong and his art to greater or lesser degrees. For those who have come to know the Master [which term is sometimes used as an alternative to the more cumbersome title of "Grandmaster" in this work, but is intended to convey equal respect and authority] or his method more recently, it is hoped that the following five observations may serve as guideposts for their Wei Kuen Do journeys:

1. Religion versus Spirituality: Grandmaster Fong makes no secret of the fact that he is an ordained minister, but Christianity—or indeed any orthodox, religious belief—has never been a requirement for membership in his system of martial arts. But here a distinction must be drawn between religion and spirituality: Orthodox religions typically require a professed belief in one or more deities and the observance of specific practices and rituals. Spirituality, by contrast, simply requires the acceptance of the idea that there is more to life than that which is physically quantifiable and empirically measurable. Like any complete martial art, Wei Kuen Do certainly has a spiritual dimension, but never one that must be expressed by affiliation with any particular faith. In the words of another great teacher, the follower of this way must simply appreciate that there is more to the arts, and indeed to life, than the fact that "rocks are hard and water is wet…"

2. Chinese versus Western: Those who have known Grandmaster Fong for any length of time are well aware of his training in both Western Boxing and various systems of Chinese Kung Fu, as well as his Chinese heritage. The casual observer of Wei Kuen Do in its most recent incarnation may initially suppose that the former art has eclipsed the latter in its founder's affections, but this would be to miss the myriad techniques and principles that owe their place in this system to the venerable Eastern martial tradition. For a start, Wei Kuen Do practitioners use every part of the fist to deliver strikes that would clearly garner a warning, and possibly even an outright disqualification, in the boxing ring. Further, just when the student thinks he may have gained a degree of control over the hand-battle, the Master's leg reminds him that there are multiple fields of engagement to be considered in this art. And be warned that a Wei Kuen Do knockout may be achieved just as well by means of a choke as a solid left hook.

3. Martial versus Art: Wei Kuen Do is a combat art, make no mistake. Anyone who has spent time in a boxing ring knows that there is nowhere to hide from the unforgiving leather and canvas in that discipline. And both the art of Wei Kuen Do itself and its senior practitioners have that same feel to them: Tough, no-nonsense and powerful. The martial pedigree of this system is indisputable. But the way Leo Fong practices and teaches his method is truly a work of art: Elegant, flowing and profound. Thus the artistry of his system is likewise undeniable. And like any true art, it is the labor of a lifetime; a relentless and rewarding quest for constant improvement and refinement.

4. Journey versus Destination: When a device malfunctions, that malfunction must be fixed. This is a correction. When a device already functions well, it may still be improved as technology advances and experience grows. This is evolution. Wei Kuen Do is an ever-evolving art. Its practitioners will never rest on their laurels, thinking that they have already discovered all there is to know. They constantly seek to improve themselves and their art, while at the same time holding fast to the core principle that, "the ultimate lies within." In this way, Wei Kuen Do is a moving target.

Master Fong trained in many different systems—both Chinese and Western—before ultimately combining their ingredients to create the art of Wei Kuen Do. And while the first formal syllabus of this system was only recently promulgated, those who know the Master and the art well also know that it will continue to evolve throughout the founder's lifetime and beyond. As a result, those who wish to follow this way can only hope to understand its trajectory, not its location, since that location is constantly on the move.

Wei Kuen Do is a journey, not a destination. In order to gather any meaningful appreciation of this art, the student must understand where it came from; the sources from which it sprang. The early chapters of this book are therefore dedicated to tracing the path that led Grandmaster Fong to create Wei Kuen Do, not only to help the student understand its rich history, but also to aid in charting its bright future...

5. Simplistic versus Simplicity: In addition to the common mistake of viewing Wei Kuen Do as a mere variant of Western Boxing, the casual observer may also be deceived by the apparent simplicity of its fundamental training tools. Comprised primarily of variations and combinations of the basic fist strikes, those who are familiar with the art's Chinese heritage may well wonder what happened to the esoteric animal hands and dramatic aerial footwork common to, say, Shaolin Kung Fu. There are at least two answers to that question:

i. Anyone with the slightest amount of sparring experience knows that it is the punch and the knee strike, not the tiger claw and the jump-spinning axe kick, that carry the day. And those who have been involved in a physical confrontation outside the relatively controlled environment of the training hall know that the only techniques that survive what Clausewitz called, "the fog of war," are those that have been practiced to the point that they have become instinctive. The Wei Kuen Do practitioner may have a more consolidated and less flashy armamentarium than some other martial artists, but he knows that he can rely on these trusty weapons under any circumstances.

WEI KUEN DO PRINCIPLE: DO NOT PRACTICE UNTIL YOU GET IT RIGHT; PRACTICE UNTIL YOU CANNOT GET IT WRONG.

ii. The novice's initial reaction to the apparent simplicity of the first few Wei Kuen Do forms will quickly be replaced by the distinct impression that they are, "bigger on the inside than they are on the outside." Their intricacy, their beauty and the secrets that lie at their core can only be detected, revealed and absorbed by dedicated practice. At each turn a new feature is exposed. On every pass another layer is discovered. As a result it is not uncommon for students to find that the Wei Kuen Do patterns take much longer to internalize than forms of similar or greater length in other systems. Keep at it. It is well worth the price of admission.

WEI KUEN DO PRINCIPLE: A GOOD TEACHER CAN ONLY SHOW YOU WHERE TO LOOK, NOT WHAT TO SEE.

III. THE ULTIMATE IS WITHIN YOU

In 1962, after many years of training in a wide variety of martial arts, Master Fong met a young Chinese man named Bruce Lee. These fellow travelers in a foreign land became fast friends and frequent training partners. One day Lee asked Fong why he had studied so many different systems of martial arts.

"To find the ultimate," Fong said.

"The ultimate is in you," Lee replied. "With your boxing skills, learn a little grappling, learn how to kick, learn some trapping and you will have the ultimate."

BRUCE LEE® and the Bruce Lee signature are registered trademarks of Bruce Lee Enterprises, LLC. The Bruce Lee name, image, likeness and all related indicia are intellectual property of Bruce Lee Enterprises, LLC. All Rights Reserved. www.brucelee.com

滙拳道

Given his religious background, the unavoidable echo for master Fong was the teaching of the apostle Luke (17:21) "...the kingdom of God is within you." The impact that this revelation had on Master Fong's martial journey cannot be overstated. It was the catalyst for the formation of the art we now know as Wei Kuen Do, and continues to be one of its bedrock principles.

WEI KUEN DO PRINCIPLE: THE ULTIMATE IS WITHIN YOU.

There are many systems, martial and otherwise, that neither require nor encourage individuality, preferring instead to replicate a single way of getting the job done each time. McDonald's restaurant, for example, strives to make every Big Mac the same, whether it is dispensed at a takeout window in Center City Philadelphia or the steadily-shuffling line of the franchise in Moscow's Pushkin Square.

If a fighting system works well for one person, shouldn't those same techniques work for another? The answer is, of course, a resounding "no." Each student has a different physique, a different psyche, different strengths and weaknesses, and, very likely, different potential fields of engagement. The six foot two police officer on the beat, for instance, will need to call upon a very different set of skills than the five foot three waitress walking home past a dark alleyway. Given the virtually infinite diversity of people and potentially infinite combinations of combat situations, a "one-size-fits-all" approach to self-defense training is less than ideal.

Moreover, to view the martial arts as nothing more than systems of self-defense is to miss entirely the beauty, the depth and indeed the very purpose of many such traditions. A few, basic self-defense moves that will suit most combat situation can be learned in a couple of weeks and proficiency with these new tools can be developed in a few months of diligent practice. The study of a true martial art, by contrast, is the journey of a lifetime. And it is important to remember that the 'lifetime' in question is that of the student, not the teacher. For the lessons, the value and the rewards of pursuing such a lifelong endeavor reside solely within you; no other person. Your teacher may rejoice in your successes and lament your failures, but in the final analysis, it is *your* life and you must lead it as you see fit.

Imagine studying under a master painter. You might ask her to teach you which paints to select and how to mix them. You would certainly learn to emulate the way in which she held and used the brush. And you would pick up scores of useful tips and tricks during your time together. But neither your goal, nor hers, would be to teach you to produce exactly the same paintings. You wouldn't even choose to mirror her style too precisely. Your ultimate goal would be to create paintings of your own design, in your own hand. They would still be paintings, of course, but they would be original compositions, not copies. For therein lies the true art.

It is the same with Wei Kuen Do. While each student's art is built upon the same foundation, the final structure should be an individual creation. Your Wei Kuen Do should no more be an exact copy of the Master's than your paintings should replicate those of your art teacher.

This is perhaps the most critical guiding principle as you start down this path. It is also the reason that the handful of blank note pages in this book are the most important ones: Because it is on these pages that you may begin to map out your own Wei Kuen Do journey, if you so choose...

WEI KUEN DO PRINCIPLE: IT IS ALL FOR YOU; MAKE IT YOUR OWN.

滙拳道

IV. GENESIS OF A WARRIOR-PRIEST

Grandmaster Tin Lung "Leo" Fong[1] was born in Canton, China on November 23, 1928 and immigrated with his family to the United States at the age of five. For many years, his father ran a small grocery store in Widener, Arkansas. Master Fong's martial arts journey began at the age of seven on the first day of school in his new country:

When young Leo returned home that day, his father asked him:

"How was school?"

Leo replied, *"Great, everybody likes me! They even sang to me: Ching Chong Chinaman..."*

With a heavy heart his father explained to him that rather than welcoming him, these cruel children had been mocking him.

The next day at recess, Leo was manning first base on the playground. One of the other kids hit a single and, while standing next to Leo, called him, "Chink." Leo punched the rude boy in the nose, knocking him to the ground! Leo was of course punished by the teacher who was supervising the game and made to stand in the hallway for two days, but, unlike his cousins who had received similar treatment and dropped out of school early on, Leo refused to accept such mistreatment. As he encountered other bullies during his school career, he continued to fight back, and, as a result, was a regular visitor at the principal's office.

---

[1] The Chinese characters for "Tin Lung" in Leo Fong's name mean: "Sky Dragon."

At this time, there were no martial arts schools in Arkansas so Leo began to study Western Boxing. At the age of twelve, he bought the book, Fundamentals of Boxing, by Barney Ross, the former World Welterweight Champion. The book only cost $1.50 from the Montgomery-Ward catalog, but paid dividends beyond imagination for the young Chinese boy. He read it from cover to cover and then hung a pillow in his bedroom to serve as a punching bag. Using this improvised training tool, Leo practiced jabs, uppercuts and hooks until the feathers flew out, swirling and spiraling around the room like snowflakes.

By studying this treatise Leo quickly learned to develop solid punching skills and was soon able to defend himself quite effectively. Among his favorite techniques were the left jab and left hook, which he continues to favor to this day. Leo learned early on that the left jab could set up an opponent for a left hook (or a right cross) very nicely, and that with those

滙拳道

three punches in combination, he could defeat just about any attacker. This, then, was Leo Fong's introduction not only to a new country, but also to a new world...

V. WESTERN BOXING

After developing his punching skills using the pillow in his bedroom, and refining them on the bullies who were foolish enough to tease him, the young Chinese fighter was eventually invited to compete in so-called "smokers"—informal boxing matches held on Friday nights in an abandoned schoolhouse. It was here that he developed his deadly left hook. In his first bout, he was matched up against the local high school quarterback. The football player was about the same height as Leo but almost fifty pounds heavier.

Leo's high school yearbook

When the bell rang, Leo charged out of his corner and start swinging like a madman. His opponent simply stepped back and hit Leo with a thunderous right hand. Leo's head bounced off the wall, and while he was not knocked out cold, the referee stopped the fight. When he got home, Leo retreated into his room and lay awake in bed trying to figure out why he had lost. Eventually it dawned on him that he had failed to consider the effect of the size differential and had been foolishly over-aggressive.

From this first fight Fong learned the importance of maintaining a proper distance and remaining patient and calm. He also began to understand that if you can learn from a loss, it's not a "loss" at all.

WEI KUEN DO PRINCIPLE: IF YOU LEARN FROM IT, IT'S NOT A LOSS.

Upon experiencing this epiphany he immediately jumped out of bed and started hitting the pillow/punching-bag again with renewed vigor. When he arrived at school the next day, several of his classmates made fun of his recent defeat. Leo did not allow his temper to get the better of him and simply informed the person who promoted these informal matches that he was keen to go again, but this time with someone closer to his own weight.

ONE OF THE MASTER'S EARLY FIGHTS

In his second match, Leo implemented the lessons he had learned from the first bout. He kept his distance and waited until his opponent attacked. Then he jabbed and stepped back; jabbed and stepped back. When the opponent moved forward again, Leo faked another jab and then hooked off the (fake) jab. His opponent dropped like a rock.

WEI KUEN DO PRINCIPLE: WHEN ANGRY, HOLD BACK YOUR FIST; WHEN STRIKING, HOLD BACK YOUR ANGER.

Fong had at least ten such informal fights before going off to Hendrix College in Conway, Arkansas to study for the ministry in 1947, where he also joined the boxing team. He received his first formal boxing lesson from, Kirby "KO" Donohoe, who was All Army Champion in World War II. In his first year of competition Leo won seven of his first eight fights and he scored five first-round knockouts, all using his increasingly deadly left hook. Unfortunately, after a year the college abandoned the program.

In Leo's second year at Hendrix College, however, the local National Guard unit invited Leo to join their team. Leo won five fights with Company "G" that year, and also reached the finals of the Arkansas State AAU Tournament. He scored one of the quickest knockouts of the tournament in his quarterfinal fight. He won the second fight by a decision, and lost in the finals in a very close decision to a boxer he had previously beaten in college competition.

CAPTAIN LEO FONG, CHAPLAIN, U.S. ARMY RESERVES

Leo continued to compete. He won two further college tournaments by knockout and made it as far as the finals in the Southwestern AAU Tournament. At this latter event Fong scored a first-round knockout in one match, won by forfeit in another but was knocked out in the finals. It was after this tournament knockout that Fong decided to retire from competition. His overall record in twenty-five formal amateur matches was 21:4—twenty-one wins, eighteen by knockout with a left hook, and four losses.

During this same time frame, however, Leo had also been called on to use his fighting prowess to defend himself on the street on several occasions. Most of these fights were ended by Fong's left hook to the jaw (a favorite target he would come to know in later years by its acupuncture designation: Stomach-5). One of his favorite techniques was to bait the opponent. On some occasions he would turn as though he was walking away, but watch the opponent's feet to see if he would take a step forward. If he did, then without even looking at his face, Leo would throw a straight right that the opponent would walk right into. When his opponent hit the ground Leo would simply walk (or run) away. A similar, favored baiting technique was to drop down as though he was going to hit the opponent in the groin or stomach and then spring up with a sizzling left to the jaw.

During the summer following Leo's retirement from competition he was hired by the Dallas Board of City Missions of the United Methodist Church to work as the athletic director at Rankin Chapel in West Dallas, Texas. There he developed a very strong boxing team and some of his students went on to win regional championships in their first year of competition, even though none of them had any boxing experiences prior to Leo's arrival.

In 1954 Leo graduated from Southern Methodist University in Dallas, Texas, and was assigned to a church in Sacramento, California.

GRADUATION FROM SOUTHERN METHODIST UNIVERSITY

There he continued to practice boxing with one of the members of the congregation who was member of the California State University Boxing Team. When the parishioner realized that his new minister was a boxer, he invited him to train at the University. Leo would go there every afternoon to train with the team and spar three rounds with each of the fighters from bantamweight to middleweight. The coach knew Fong as friend of the parishioner, and all that sparring kept the young minister in fighting shape, so this practice continued until the parishioner graduated and Leo shifted his martial studies from boxing to Jujitsu and Judo, but it is undeniably Western Boxing that formed the first pillar of the edifice that was to become Wei Kuen Do.

ANYTHING GOES, ALMOST — Leo Agbulos (left) former local professional lightweight boxer of some note, will face Byung Yu of Korea next Saturday in a special full-contact karate match in Civic Auditorium. Above, Agbulos is shown working out with Leo Fong, head of the local Tae Kwan Do Karate School. Clothing is optional and Agbulos will wear trunk, no shoes. Byung Yu is slated to be dressed in karate style, but both will use 8-ounce gloves. The fighters may punch, kick, or use their elbows and knees to the advantage. It will be a 6-round match part of the Captain Weber Days Karate Championships.

One might well expect that a Chinese-born boy in search of a method of self-defense would naturally have begun with the Eastern martial arts. But in young Leo's place and time of need, the Western methodology was the only system available. It was in the ring, and not on the mat, then, that the future master began to hone his art. Rather than practicing the myriad techniques common to many styles of Kung Fu, Fong focused his attention on a handful of methods and trajectories for delivering a simple punch. To paraphrase Bruce Lee, rather than trying to learn ten thousand techniques, he practiced these few technique ten thousand times. And it is the fist—in its many incarnations—that stands as the first and most powerful weapon in the armamentarium of the Wei Kuen Do practitioner.

☯ **The Fundamentals:** How to form the fist, how to deliver a blow without hurting the hand, how to retract to guard position, and so on…

☯ **The Falling Step:** The idea here is to land the punch a fraction of a second before the lead foot touches the ground. This allows the fighter to move forward so as to close the interval, and at the same time put the weight of the body behind the strike.

☯ **The Power of the Hook Punch:** Experience teaches that a disproportionately high number of knockouts in the ring, and elsewhere, are achieved by applying rotational, rather than frontal, force to the opponent's skull. The twisting motion required to accomplish this feat is most easily produced with a hook punch to the opponent's chin. Unlike a haymaker, that follows a wide, shallow curve from launch to impact point, however, the hook does not telegraph its intent; rather it tracks a fairly straight line until the last moment, when it swerves in sharply toward its target.

☯ **Combinations:** No matter how powerful a particular punch may be, unless it happens to land perfectly each and every time it is attempted, it will likely have to learn to work in combination with other techniques. And while this principle may be simple in theory, it is demanding in practice, for the only way to ensure that combinations of techniques will survive in the crucible of combat is to drill them over and over and over again, until the body, and not just the mind, has absorbed them.

BOXING'S "BIG THREE"

A devotee of the sweet science and an avid student of the tale of the tape, Master Fong frequently makes reference to lessons learned from particular boxers, and even cites specific matches that serve to illustrate his point. In this context he refers affectionately to boxing's "Big Three:" Sergio Martinez, Manny Pacquiao and Floyd Mayweather.

☯ **On Footwork:** Fong cites **Sergio Martinez**—who dropped in to observe a Wei Kuen Do training session on a California beach during the first international convention in the autumn of 2012—as a master of footwork; a skill that likely took root during his days as a soccer star. It is this ability that accounts for Martinez's explosive speed when, "closing the gap," as seen, for example, in his one-punch knockout of Paul Williams in 2011. The importance of this kind of footwork is evident in WKD's trademark, "V-step."

BOXING LEGEND SERGIO MARTINEZ DROPS BY…

● **On Offense:** In watching **Manny Pacquiao**, Master Fong notes the importance of being able to launch an attack from different angles, and also knowing how to sustain an attack while moving from side to side, thereby negating the opponent's ability to counter. The application of these principles is manifested in WKD's, "Angles of Attack."

● **On Defense:** From the fighting style of **Floyd Mayweather**, Master Fong gleaned various defensive skills, including shoulder rolls and evasive techniques. In particular Fong commends Mayweather's ability to gauge distance and to hit without getting hit back. The power of these techniques can be seen at work in WKD's "Circles of Destruction."

THE BIG THREE: SERGIO MARTINEZ, MANNY PACQUIAO AND FLOYD MAYWEATHER

● **On Cross-Training:** There can be no doubt that Western Boxing is a central figure in the art of Wei Kuen Do, but Master Fong's creation is a mosaic, not a portrait. Its components are legion, and they are drawn from a wide variety of martial, and non-martial, realms. For example, in addition to those fighting systems chronicled in greater detail below, Fong drew some of his inspiration from sports like basketball and football.

LEO FONG'S COLLEGE FOOTBALL TEAM

WKD was inspired by many sources, such as basketball fakes and the evasiveness of touch football, which I gleaned from my college years as a running back in the touch football league. Cross-training and cross-knowledge is a valuable tool in completing the WKD mosaic. The ultimate fighting approach is not about learning ten different styles, but integrating all key elements into one working and functional unit, much like a well-trained army. That is the essence and evolutionary process of WKD. Always evolving. Constantly on the growing edge. Always striving but never arriving. –GMLF

VI. JUDO, WRESTLING, TANG SOO DO, JUJITSU

In 1954 the Eastern martial arts were still in their infancy in the United States and good instructors—especially those who were permanent fixtures in the community—were hard to find. As a result, many martial artists who came up during these exciting times had no choice but to take advantage of whatever training was available, when and where they could find it. Leo Fong was no exception. Both his passion for the martial arts in their infinite diversity, and the changing landscape and availability of high quality teachers, launched Fong into a decade-long cross-training adventure that covered many, if not most, of the major martial arts systems.

After his parishioner and training partner left the California State University Boxing Team, Fong began studying with Bill Luke, a student of Judo Pioneer Bruce Tegner. Tegner was from Ventura, California, and owned a publishing company called, "Thor Publications." His extensive library contained many practitioners' first reference works on a wide variety of martial arts.

After a few years Luke too left Sacramento to move to Los Angeles, so Fong joined the Sacramento YMCA and continued training in Judo with Bob Bendicts. While in the Judo program at the YMCA, Fong met a man named Frank Lawrence who was a former member of the San Jose State University Wrestling Team. Bendicts was teaching a Wrestling class at the YMCA and Fong cross-trained in the two grappling arts for a time. He also cross-trained in the art of Jujitsu during these formative years.

A few years after that Fong switched again to Kung Fu [detailed in the following chapters] and Tang Soo Do. It was at the California State University at Sacramento that Fong met Korean Karate expert Chong Yuk Yong, of the Moo Duk Kwan. The two men—together with two other friends who were members of the Sacramento Fire Department—began training regularly in so-called Korean Karate in the fellowship hall of Leo's church.

Yong was a private student of Master Hwang Kee, the head of the Moo Duk Kwan Association. When Chong Yuk Yong graduated from University, Fong decided to focus on his martial studies on Kung Fu, but sometime after Yong returned to Korea, he submitted a request to promote Fong to First Degree Black Belt. When the certificate arrived, it made Fong an official member of the Moo Duk Kwan Association. He was overwhelmed by this honor and never forgot the lessons he learned in this ancient and venerable art. And so it was that elements of Judo, Wrestling and Tang Soo Do were among the first ingredients in the recipe of Wei Kuen Do.

MASTER HWANG KEE

☯ **Throws:** Judo, Jujitsu and Western Wrestling all teach various ways of using momentum and balance to throw one's opponent, and while these techniques may not be considered "core curriculum" in Wei Kuen Do, they definitely comprise part of it martial armamentarium.

☯ **Locks:** Joint locks—sometimes taught as bone-breaking techniques—have long been part of the classical martial tradition, and feature in Wei Kuen Do when fighting in grappling range.

☯ **Chokes:** Choking an opponent to unconsciousness is one of the fastest, surest, and some argue most controlled, ways of ending a fight. Fong learned these powerful tools in his Jujitsu and Judo training, and endorses their use under appropriate circumstances.

● **Kicks:** Tang Soo Do is known for its high kicking techniques. While there are no kicks above the waist in Wei Kuen Do, having the flexibility and strength to deliver these spectacular high kicks ensures that their more down-to-earth cousins are that much more powerful and accurate.

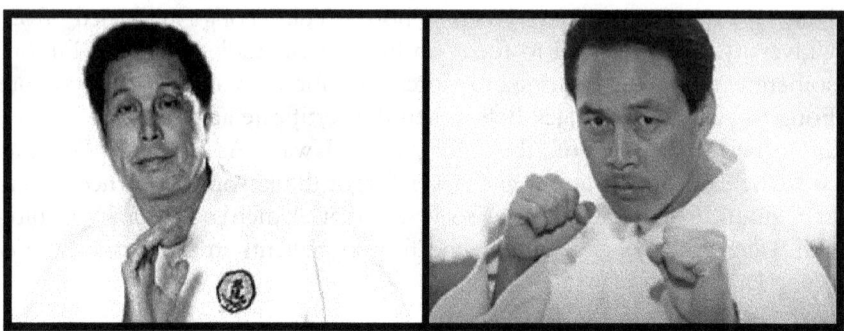

PROFESSOR WALLY JAY   PROFESSOR LEON JAY

Decades later, the influence of Jujitsu on Leo Fong and his art was to re-assert itself. During the 1980s and beyond, Fong joined forces with the founder of Small Circle Jujitsu—Professor Wally Jay—and two other noted martial arts masters—Modern Arnis founder Remy Presas and Karate expert George Dillman—to form a kind of Council of Masters, sharing techniques, ideas and students all around the world. Leon Jay— the present headmaster of the Small Circle system—remembers both his father's and his own experiences with Leo Fong:

THE PROFESSORS JAY
My father, who taught seminars with Leo for many years, had the highest respect for him. When I trained with him for the first time myself I remember being very impressed with his physical skill and fitness. It was only later that I learned his actual age and was quite surprised and that much more impressed at the superb shape he was in! Leo is a world class martial artist and will always be a friend of the Jay family. —Leon Jay

滙拳道

VII. CHOY LAY FUT KUNG FU

Having developed phenomenal hand techniques, refined them in the crucible of combat as a competitive boxer, and then augmented these core hand skills with locks, throws and chokes learned on the Judo/Jujitsu/Wrestling mat, Leo Fong next set his sights on learning a traditional Chinese system of self-defense. For a Chinese born fighter, this was a homecoming of sorts.

While traveling through San Francisco's Chinatown one day in 1958, Leo had a chance encounter with an elderly Chinese man who was standing on the street corner. Leo asked the man whether there were any Kung Fu schools in the area. The old man replied, "There's one near the park and another up there near the Baptist Church." Leo asked which was better and the elderly gentleman merely laughed. "It's up to you. An old man runs the one near the park. The one up by the church is run by a younger man." Leo decided to try the older teacher because he concluded that with age would come experience. It was through this series of coincidences that Leo was fortunate enough to discover and train under Choy Lay Fut Grandmaster Lau Bun.

GRANDMASTER LAU BUN

WEI KUEN DO PRINCIPLE: EXPERIENCE IS THE BEST TEACHER.

Fong made his way to the location near the park that the old man had described and found himself in a cellar basement kwoon. Grandmaster Lau Bun's attention was focused elsewhere when Leo first walked in, but after a lengthy wait, Lau Bun turned his attention to his young visitor and began to interrogate him about his reasons for wanting to learn Kung Fu. Over the course of perhaps half an hour Leo explained that he had begun his martial arts journey in order to protect himself, had tested his mettle in several styles, but was now looking for the ultimate form of self-defense. Lau Bun, apparently satisfied with Leo's explanation, agreed to teach him, so for several years following that auspicious day, Leo commuted regularly to San Francisco to train with this legendary master.

The Choy Lay Fut (also rendered, "Choy Li Fut") [蔡李佛] system was founded in 1836 by Chan Heung, a native of China's Guangdong province. As a young martial artist Chan Heung trained under at least five different masters, and eventually combined the knowledge he had absorbed into his own style, named to honor his teachers: The Buddhist monk **Choy** Fook who taught him Choy Gar, **Li** Yau-San who taught him Li Gar; and his uncle Chan Yuen-Wu, who taught him **Fut** Gar.

Choy Lay Fut is a composite system, comprised of aspects of various other styles. In addition to the powerful arm and hand techniques adopted from the Shaolin animal forms, Lau Bun taught Leo that mastery of the horse stance was a vital component, and necessary prerequisite, to progressing in the art. In fact, students were not permitted to study hand techniques until they had first mastered this stance. As a result, in the course of his training Leo often practiced the horse (stance) form for hours at a time.

> Choy Li Fut is the most effective system that I've seen for fighting more than one person. [It] is one of the most difficult styles to attack and defend against. Choy Li Fut is the only style [of Kung Fu] that traveled to Thailand to fight the Thai boxers and hadn't lost. —Bruce Lee

Training in Choy Lay Fut gave Leo his first real exposure to the use of kicking and hand techniques not permitted in boxing or taught in Judo/Jujitsu. The impact that exposure to this new universe of striking and blocking possibilities had on the young martial artist cannot be underestimated. To this day, in fact, Wei Kuen Do retains various techniques and principles of Choy Lay Fut:

☯ **Kicks:** Both Choy Lay Fut and Wei Kuen Do employ low kicking techniques (below the opponent's waist) in combat.

☯ **Hand Techniques:** Choy Lay Fut's frequent use of the backfist, the uppercut and the open hand blocking method are also integral to Wei Kuen Do.

☯ **Push-pull:** While not unique to Choy Lay Fut, the principle that when pushed by the opponent, the practitioner should pull, and vice versa, is fundamental to both self-defense methods.

☯ **Whipping:** A method where the practitioner's upper torso twists to generate more power in executing hand and arm techniques is common to both systems.

☯ **Angling:** Holding the torso at an angle to the opponent to reduce the exposed target area while allowing greater reach with the lead arm is employed in both styles.

WEI KUEN DO

> The dragon and tiger met as the wind and the cloud.
> 龍虎風雲會
> My disciple, you must take good care of your future.
> 徒兒好自為
> To revive the arts of Shaolin,
> 重光少林術
> Don't let future generations forget about this teaching.
> 世代毋相遺
>
> —Poem given to Chan Heung by his master Choy Fook

滙拳道

VIII. SIL LUM KUNG FU

Never one to give less than one hundred percent, while training in Choy Lay Fut with Grandmaster Lau Bun, Leo and his training buddy, Jimmy Ong, decided to check out the other school recommended by the elderly man during the chance encounter on the street corner: the Sil Lim school of Tim Yuen ("T.Y.") Wong. The two young martial artists went to the Sil Lum school one evening and saw a student standing in front of the mirror doing forms with small dumbbells in his hands. When the student finished, he turned around and introduced himself to the visitors. His name was James Yimm Lee (who would one day be the co-founder the Jun Fan Gung Fu Institute in Oakland and one of only three instructors certified by Bruce Lee).

GRANDMASTER TIM YUEN WONG

After talking with the two young martial artists for a while, James Lee invited them both to join the Sil Lum school. While Jimmy Ong declined the invitation, Leo accepted and so began a friendship with James Lee that would one day lead to Leo's first encounter with Bruce Lee. In terms of his Sil Lum training, however, Leo continued to cross-train at T.Y. Wong's school until Wong and James Lee had a falling out (over ten dollars!) which prompted Lee to quit the school and open one of his own. But therein lies another story…

Sil Lum (in Cantonese or "Shaolin" in the Mandarin dialect) [少林寺] Kung Fu is perhaps the best known of the Chinese martial arts, at least in part as a result of the wildly successful television and film portrayals of the Shaolin Temple in China's Henan province and the martial skills of the warrior-monks who trained there. It is based in large part on the ancient animal forms. The art that Leo studied at T.Y. Wong's school in the late 1950s and early 1960s can be traced directly back to the legendary Shaolin Temple.

THE SHAOLIN TEMPLE

Around the turn of the Twentieth Century a monk named Leong Sil Jong, who had studied at the Shaolin Temple for over fifty years, left this holy ground and moved to Woung-Nam province. There, he met a wealthy nobleman who asked him to teach martial arts to his sickly son, Hue Lung

Gong. In exchange, the nobleman built a martial arts school for Leong Sil Jong. Jong did as the father asked and taught Kung Fu to the son for many years. Jong also had a nephew—Leong Tin Chee—who studied the Shaolin arts under both Hue Lung Gong (who went on to become a teacher in his own right) and others.

Leong Tin Chee went on to win a nationwide sparring tournament sponsored by the government in order to find the best martial arts masters for instructing the Chinese military. One of Chee's students was Wong Tim Yuen ("T.Y. Wong") who, after studying with master Chee for ten years, emigrating to America, taking with him the seeds of the Shaolin arts. And it was at T.Y. Wong's Sil Lum school—the first of its kind in the United States—that Leo Fong studied for many years. From his Sil Lum training Leo learned many principles and techniques that were eventually absorbed into the WKD syllabus:

● **Hand Techniques:** Sil Lum practitioners frequently use the hammerfist as well as the open hand blocking method previously mentioned in connection with Choy Lay Fut. Both of these feature in the syllabus of Wei Kuen Do.

● **Kicks:** Like Choy Lay Fut, Sil Lum also employs the low kicking techniques (below the opponent's waist) that are taught in Wei Kuen Do.

● **Pliability:** Sil Lum means, "young forest;" an allusion to the pliability and resilience of new-growth trees. Both this art and Wei Kuen Do emphasize the importance of these characteristics in the practitioner and the art.

● **Fitness:** Anyone who has witnessed students training in the Shaolin/Sil Lum arts can attest to the fact that there is a tremendous emphasis on fitness. Leo Fong's physical prowess—even today—is legendary. To this day he continues the practice of working out with hand weights; a training method he first learned from James Lee at the Sil Lum school of T.Y. Wong.

● **Repetition:** In the introduction to his book on Sil Lum Kung Fu, Master Fong writes, *"Remember: the effectiveness of Sil Lum Kung Fu depends upon split-second timing and reflexive action, which are achieved only through repetitious practice."* The importance of repetition in Wei Kuen Do—and indeed any other art—cannot be overemphasized. The practice of a given technique or form moves through several stages:

1. **Comprehension:** The student can mimic the form.
2. **Memorization:** The student can do the form without a model.
3. **Understanding:** The student begins to grasp the form's meaning.
4. **Internalization:** The student's body begins to 'learn' the form through muscle memory.
5. **Instinct:** The student's body knows the form so well that it performs automatically. It is only at the fifth and final stage that the technique may be relied upon under pressure. And this level of competence can be achieved only by endless repetition…

WEI KUEN DO PRINCIPLE: THE PERFECT STRIKE IS INSTINCTIVE.

滙拳道

IX. ARNIS/ESCRIMA

In 1974, Leo received a call from a producer in the Philippines who had read his martial arts books and seen Leo on the cover of *Black Belt* magazine. The producer offered Leo the lead role in two of his upcoming films. At first, Leo declined the offer, but eventually accepted, and traveled to the Philippines to begin filming his first movie: "Murder in the Orient" (also released under the title: "Manila Gold"). Leo was treated like a star in the Philippines, and even after filming was complete he decided to remain for another year. It was during this time that Leo became a close friend and student of Remy Presas, the founder of Modern Arnis.

GRANDMASTERS REMY PRESAS AND LEO FONG TRAINING IN THE PHILIPPINES

Even after Leo returned to California, he continued to study the Filipino cane and empty hand arts by becoming a student of Angel Cabales, the founder of Serrada Escrima. Over the years Leo developed his own style of stick fighting which he called, "Modern Escrima." And while the art of Wei Kuen Do had already begun taking shape before Master Fong began training in Arnis/Escrima, true to form he incorporated what he found useful into his existing styles. As a result, the influence of these cane arts on Wei Kuen Do and Modern Escrima in their current forms, is clear. In fact, Leo attributes the structure of his entire martial arts curriculum to Angel Cabales, because Angel was so skilled at creating a system that was both simple and easy to grasp, but at the same time rich in depth and complexity.

GRANDMASTERS ANGEL CABALES AND LEO FONG

◎ **Footwork:** As a threshold matter, Leo Fong integrated the footwork of the Filipino arts directly into his system(s) of self-defense.

◎ **The Cane as a Training Tool:** Master Fong routinely uses the cane as a training tool. On some occasions its heft is employed as a hand-weight. On others, a padded cane is used as a fast-moving striking target ("Focus Sticks"). In addition, as in most weapon arts, many techniques with the cane have empty hand translations, and practice with the weapon teaches principles and patterns that can be applied to devastating effect when employed in unarmed combat.

滙拳道

From the on guard (1), Anthony Davis attacks with an overhead right. Leo Fong steps to the side and with the left hand directs Davis' force forward (2). Fong counterattacks Davis' wrist (3). Fong follows through with a strike to the elbow (4) and continues with a strike to the chin (5).

◉ **The Cane as a Weapon:** The cane is one of the best weapons to learn for self-defense purposes, if for no other reason than so many common items—umbrellas, walking sticks, towel racks and so on—can be easily substituted in an emergency for the rattan original.

WEI KUEN DO

☯ **The Flow:** On a broader and deeper level, the relaxed flow and latitude for variation encouraged in the Filipino arts is the *sine qua non* of Wei Kuen Do.

☯ **Attitude:** Those who had the privilege of training with both Leo Fong and the late Remy Presas will immediately recognize certain similarities: Positive and enthusiastic attitudes toward teaching the martial arts; tolerance and appreciation of variety in the approaches taken by their students; and an overarching commitment to the proposition that training in the martial arts should make practitioners better, happier and more well-rounded people.

WEI KUEN DO PRINCIPLE: ATTITUDE IS THE MOST IMPORTANT SKILL.

MODERN ESCRIMA'S BASIC STRIKES

❶❷ Stick Hook: twist palm up to left temple, palm down to right temple.
❸❹ Stick Chop: chop down to opponents collar bone, left and right.
⑤ Stick Jab: jab with a twist of the wrist, palm up or down, to solar plexus.
⑥⑦ Stick Jab: jab with a twist of the wrist, palm up or down, under pectoral muscle, left and right.
⑧⑨ Stick Strike: strike to shin bone, left and right.
⑩⑪ Stick Jab: jab with a twist of the wrist, palm up or down, to eyes, left and right.
⑫ Stick Jab: jab with a twist of the wrist, palm up or down, to throat.
⓭⓮ Stick Strike: strike to hip bone, wrist bone, knuckles, left and right.

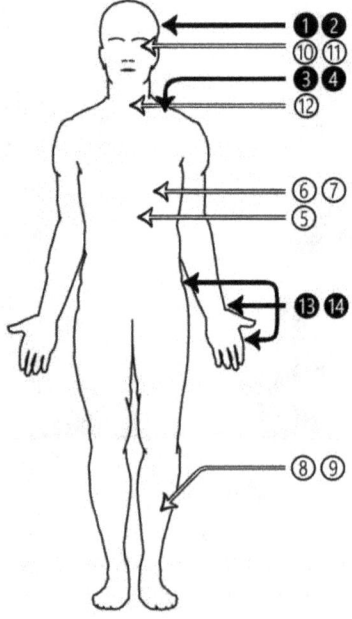

● **Practice Pointer:** The "short striking" of Modern Escrima employs limited movements so as to avoid telegraphing, and a single, shorter cane.

● **Practice Pointer:** Among the innovations of Modern Arnis is *avoiding* striking the hands. Modern Escrima, by contrast, *emphasizes* striking the hand, the wrist and the knuckles when appropriate (e.g. #3 and #4).

● **Practice Pointer:** While Modern Arnis and Modern Escrima share some techniques, others appear only in the Modern Escrima syllabus, such as the groin strike (#10), the arch block and the retracting block.

● **Practice Pointer:** Strike #13 was derived from a technique perfected by Angel Cabales, who used to perform a unique, overhead cane attack with a rotation that made it appear that the stick *came out of nowhere...*

WEI KUEN DO

![Photo sequence]

"LEO FONG'S SHORT STRIKE ESCRIMA," *INSIDE KUNG FU* MAGAZINE, NOVEMBER 2003

MODERN ESCRIMA

X. JEET KUNE DO

When James Lee left the Sil Lum school after falling out with T.Y. Wong, he started teaching martial arts classes in his garage in Oakland, and invited Leo to attend. Fong trained with Lee until 1962 at which time when James told Leo about a young Kung Fu expert named Bruce Lee. Fong was introduced to Lee at Wally Jay's Annual Luau in Oakland, and any doubts about the brash young newcomer's abilities were quickly dispelled by the speed and explosiveness of his demonstration at that event.

BRUCE LEE® and the Bruce Lee signature are registered trademarks of Bruce Lee Enterprises, LLC.
The Bruce Lee name, image, likeness and all related indicia are intellectual property of Bruce Lee Enterprises, LLC.
All Rights Reserved. www.brucelee.com

WEI KUEN DO

The two Chinese martial artists quickly became friends and frequent training partners. Over the years that followed Lee and Fong spent a great deal of time practicing, writing and discussing the martial arts, and while it is true that Leo learned a great many things from Bruce, the reverse is also true. In this way their relationship is perhaps better characterized as that of colleagues rather than teacher and student. As a result, it is no surprising that Jeet Kune Do and Wei Kuen Do share many common techniques and principles [note that Masters Lee and Fong render the Chinese word for "fist" with a slightly different English spelling]:

- **Kicks:** Like most of the arts discussed so far, Jeet Kune Do and Wei Kuen Do both employ low kicking techniques despite the fact that the founders of both styles were quite capable of delivering much higher leg techniques with blinding speed.

- **Hand Techniques:** As discussed above, both styles rely heavily on Western Boxing strikes, particularly the straight lead punch; a feature of Jeet Kune Do that has a great deal to do with the Fong-Lee interaction.

- **The Metaphor of Water:** The Masters of both arts frequently use the metaphor or water, urging their students to learn to move and behave like this elemental substance.

- **Economy of Motion:** Both styles prize efficiency, directness and simplicity. There is a direct correlation between the number and complexity of techniques taught, and the amount of time the practitioner has to devote to each. As a result, focusing more attention on a smaller collection of moves will produce proficiency much faster than will splitting that same amount of attention over a much wider and more complex syllabus.

- **Centerline Theory:** The center line in centerline theory refers to an imaginary line running down the center of the body. The idea is to exploit, control and dominate the opponent's center line. Attacks, defenses and footwork are all designed to protect the practitioner's center line and open the opponent's. The three primary rules for applying this theory are:

1. He who controls the centerline, controls the fight.
2. Protect your own center line and control/exploit the opponent's.
3. Control the center line by occupying it.

滙拳道

XI. THE LEE-FONG CONNECTION

Bruce Lee and Leo Fong each had a significant impact on the other's martial journey during the time that they walked this path together. As discussed above, many aspects of Lee's style are evident in Fong's Wei Kuen Do. At the same time, Lee was impressed by Fong's boxing abilities and added boxing punches, stances and other principles to his art. When the two first met in the class in James Lee's garage, Bruce favored a classic Wing Chun stance (lead hand high and the rear hand low, by the solar plexus). When Fong told Lee that he preferred the modern American boxing stance, with his lead hand low and his rear hand by his cheek, Lee took one look and said, "I like it because I can't trap you lead hand." Over the next few years, Bruce Lee completely changed his primary fighting stance and eventually adopted more of a boxing stance as his own.

WEI KUEN DO

Similarly, after Lee's legendary grudge match with Wong Jack Mon, he called Fong on the telephone and said, "Man I need more angles. The forward blast is limited against a mobile target." Fong responded by suggesting the use of more boxing strikes: Hooks, uppercuts and crosses. The following week, when Fong arrived at James Lee's garage for their regular training session, Lee was practicing a repertoire of boxing punches just as Leo had suggested. In this way Fong witnessed—and indeed contributed—to the birth of Jeet Kune Do.

While it is clear that these two Chinese immigrant martial artists had a significant effect on each other's technical repertoires, perhaps the most profound impact that Lee had on Fong was in the realm of ideas and philosophy. Given the vital importance of Bruce Lee's observation to Leo Fong regarding the fact that the ultimate art may be found in each of us, that story is retold here in Master Fong's own words:

> *My epiphany came when one night while 'slumming' in San Francisco for some martial arts action. Bruce and I talked about the many styles of martial arts that I was doing. He asked me a pointed question: "Why in the hell are you training in so many styles of martial arts?" I replied, "Bruce, I want to find the ultimate martial art." He looked at me, cracked a smile, pushed my chest with his fingers and said, "Man, the ultimate is in here. Take your boxing skills and expand on them with kicking, grappling, trapping and punching." That changed not only martial arts life; it changed my life in general. It gave me a new perspective in how to look at developing skills in everything. Prior to meeting Bruce I did not know how to integrate. I would go to the gym and lift weights for hours, several times a week. Every other day I would practice the Korean Karate kata. On alternate days I would practice the Kung Fu Forms. And still I had to spend time on shadow boxing, sparring and hitting the heavy bag. I had no time to do anything else! My training encompassed Tae Kwan Do, Boxing, Karate, Choy Lay Fut Kung Fu, Sil Lum Kung Fu, and occasionally some Judo and Wrestling. I felt like a guy traveling on a long trip overloaded with luggage. After Bruce Lee's pivotal statement, "Man, it's in here...." I began to think in terms of how to absorb techniques and make them work in all situations. And it began with my boxing roots. —GMLF*

In addition to Lee's revelatory injunction to Fong to the effect that the ultimate art lies within, he also illustrated by both word and deed that the path to mastery lies not in seeking to be like the great masters, but rather in seeking what the great masters sought. It was a lesson that Fong would never forget, and indeed incorporated into the fundamental building blocks of WKD philosophy.

WEI KUEN DO PRINCIPLE: DO NOT MERELY SEEK TO BE LIKE THE WISE MASTERS; SEEK WHAT THEY SOUGHT.

滙拳道

The person who is best situated to describe the relationship between Bruce Lee and Leo Fong, however, is Linda Lee-Cadwell; Bruce's wife.

LINDA LEE-CADWELL AND LEO FONG

BRUCE LEE AND LEO FONG

Bruce and I first met Leo Fong in 1964 at Wally Jay's annual luau. We had just moved from Seattle to California and were living at James Lee's house in Oakland. At that time Bruce and James were working out in James' garage, and were in the process of opening a school together. Leo already had a martial arts background when he met Bruce so they each had things to show the other, and they quickly became colleagues and friends. Bruce had great respect for Leo—for his knowledge as well as his personality. They would talk about martial arts for many hours, often long into the night!

Bruce was a unique individual and had so many things to share with those who had previously trained with traditional masters. A frequently quoted encounter between Bruce and Leo occurred when Bruce asked Leo why he was training in so many different styles.

Leo replied, "I am looking for the ultimate martial art."
Bruce responded by saying, "The ultimate is in you."

I believe that Leo took this advice to heart. Bruce used to say: "We are all born with two legs and two arms—how many different ways can there be to accomplish your goals in the martial arts?" Because Leo was also a minister, he was able to understand that this advice could apply equally to the search for spiritual meaning within. In fact, the duality of Leo's dual roles as a minister and a fighter may very likely have been one ingredient in Bruce's idea to tell the story of a wandering martial monk in the old American West.

Bruce worked with Leo to help start his writing and acting careers. He was always keen to encourage others to "express themselves," and to do so honestly. He once stayed up all night with Leo to help him complete one of his books and he also arranged for Leo to appear on the cover of Black Belt Magazine in 1970.

Bruce and Leo were both extremely well-rounded martial artists. One of the passions they shared was fitness. You could tell just by looking at them and the way they moved. In this way they were both ahead of their time. Both Leo and Bruce had experience in and an appreciation of Western boxing. Bruce used to study footage of boxing matches, but he would reverse the film so as to be able to view the boxers fighting with their right sides forward.

They also shared a belief in the importance of philosophy and spirituality in the martial arts and life in general. I think it is wonderful that Bruce is now almost as well-known for his philosophical ideas as his martial prowess. Bruce continually searched out the writings of philosophers—ancient and modern, Eastern and Western—and also wrote about his own thoughts in this regard. He was always engaged in the process of self-improvement; of becoming who he was. He never reached a point where he felt that he had learned everything there was to know about a particular subject.

People sometimes misunderstand the essence of Jeet Kune Do. Students can't simply study many different martial arts, figure out what works best for them, and then call it "Jeet Kune Do." The first step is to learn and understand what Bruce was doing when he was developing and practicing his art. I know that Leo would agree because he was there at the time that the art was evolving. For example, it was around that time that Bruce had a famous fight with another, well-known Chinese martial artist. While Bruce prevailed in this encounter, it was a turning point in his development. It was really the genesis of Jeet Kune Do. While Bruce never

> lost his love of Wing Chun, he realized that he needed to expand upon what he had previously learned, and began to focus even more intently on fitness, speed and strength training.
>
> Those martial artists who make a real effort to discover the essence of what Bruce was doing and include it in their art are the ones who will truly preserve and carry on the art of Jeet Kune Do. Bruce knew Leo to be a man of integrity who would not corrupt his work, and Leo has contributed so much to the martial arts. He certainly deserves a place of honor in the constellation of noted martial artists. Bruce would have approved.
>
> To Leo and his students, I would say this: Thank you for the honor and respect you have paid to Bruce and his art of Jeet Kune Do. Bruce and Leo were fortunate to share a unique friendship based on their ability to honestly express their thoughts to each other about the meaning of life. The study of the martial arts has been a spiritual journey for both Bruce and Leo as I can see from the process Leo has experienced in developing his art of Wei Kuen Do. I know that all of Bruce's and Leo's students worldwide appreciate the gift they have received from these two outstanding martial artists, and understand their responsibility to carry their message to future generations.
>
> —Linda Lee-Cadwell

Shortly before Bruce Lee died he told his students to stop using the name Jeet Kune Do and to "find their own truth." He did this in part because his name—and the name of his art—were being increasingly appropriated by those who had no proper basis for doing so, but also because he firmly believed that walking the martial path should be a personal journey. He told his followers in no uncertain terms that they should not seek to imitate him, but rather should seek their own way of expressing themselves through their martial studies.

While Leo Fong has never claimed to be a Jeet Kune Do instructor, his common ancestry, time spent training and ideological connection with the late Bruce Lee supports the proposition that Wei Kuen Do may be quite similar to the system into which Lee's Jeet Kune Do would eventually have evolved if its founder had not been taken from the world at such a young age.

GUTEI POINTS AT THE MOON

Gutei was a wise Zen master. One day a student asked him the secret of enlightenment. Gutei simply pointed at the moon. The next day, the student told his friends that he had discovered old Gutei's secret. When they asked him what it was, he held up his finger, for he had only seen the finger, and not the moon…

Lee,

Received your book by Perlo, will read it soon. As for ▓▓▓▓ some people would do anything to get publicity. Or he actually think a non-athlete can out-gun a trained one with "doubtful" quickies———

Silent Flute is moving along fine, we ran into some problem in location, but we should know real soon on the official date.

More exciting still are several developing possibilities which I will tell you when the moment comes.

I love to use your "drawing course" — in fact, I was thinking at one time of joining, but if you have it, fine!

Due to my back, I have to say I am not in my best of shape; however, my JKD is something else — with adversity you are shocked to higher levels, much like a rain storm that is so violent, but yet afterwards all plant grows. More and more I pity the martial artists that are blinded by their partiality and ignorance.

Will do an article for Black Belt as soon as I can find time. The India trip wipe me out. By the way, hope your book will do good. If there is any help I can render for your future book, feel free to ask.

Got to go now, say hello to your wife for me and take care.

XII. THE WAY OF THE INTEGRATED FIST

> A gentle breeze carried the scent of the wolf pack downwind to a meadow where a cat and fox sat talking. "Wolves," remarked the fox nonchalantly, "I know a thousand ways to get away from them," for he was very boastful. The fox began enumerating all of his various evasion tactics. By and by the cat called down from the tree he had just climbed, "I only know one," but it was too late—the pack had fallen on the fox and he could no longer hear... —<u>Kishido: The Way of the Western Warrior</u>

From his discussions with Bruce Lee, Leo Fong came to recognize that seeking to add together all the techniques and forms he had learned in the various martial arts he had studied had in fact bogged him down with too much "martial baggage." He therefore resolved to begin "traveling light;" to simplify; to integrate the useful elements of each component system until he had reduced his art to the essential "bare bones." And the first few building blocks of his new system were lessons learned in the boxing ring.

> *It began with my boxing roots: I remembered my left hook and how I had knocked out eighteen opponents with it. I thought of one of my colleagues, an outstanding professional boxer by the name of Billy Walker. He was from North Little Rock, Arkansas. Billy had only one punch. It was a left hook. While sharing a dressing room one day I said to him, "Billy you only have one punch; a left hook. Your opponents know what you are going to do, so why is it that you manage to knock most them out?" He looked me in the face, smiled and said, "They don't when in the hell its coming!"*
>
> *At that moment I understood. I realized that it is not quantity but quality that counts. The same was true of an outstanding amateur flyweight boxer I met once by the name of Bill Malone. He was Arkansas AAU champion in 1947. I sparred with him one afternoon and I could not touch him. All he used was a left jab. He would jab and move, move and jab. I had seen this principle at play in the boxing ring, but it was Bruce Lee who crystallized this idea in my mind. —GMLF*

滙拳道

WEI KUEN DO PRINCIPLE: DON'T JUST ACCUMULATE; INTEGRATE.

So Master Fong began with the fist. Not just the punch in its straight, hook, and uppercut incarnations, but also the backfist, hammerfist and axefist, all of which employ striking surfaces that would be illegal in Western Boxing. These six hand techniques are at the core of the practice of Wei Kuen Do, but it is not nearly enough to know how to perform them. They must be drilled thousands upon thousands of times, practiced against shadows, leather and flesh, called upon when exhausted or surprised, to the point that they become instinctive and automatic. Only when these hand techniques are as natural to the practitioner as the act of breathing can they be truly be said to have been mastered.

Because Wei Kuen Do is a total body art, it also embraces kicking techniques, but they are few in number and always delivered below the waist. The four primary kicks are: The front kick, the side kick, the hook kick and the sweep kick. This is not to say that the Wei Kuen Do practitioner cannot employ other leg techniques—in the practice of Wei Kuen Do there are many "right" answers and few "wrong" ones—but rather that even standing alone, these four primary leg techniques will serve the practitioner well in almost any encounter. And, as with their manual counterparts, these kicks must be practiced to the point that they have been completely internalized if they are to be of any use at all in combat.

Once the Wei Kuen Do practitioner has a good sense the primary techniques, he begins to practice them in combinations and patterns. And just as the goal is for the techniques themselves to become instinctive, so should the forms in which they are combined. The first set of these is known as, "The Ten Angles of Attack." In these forms, the practitioner learns to deploy his hand weapons in a variety of combinations, against a variety of attacks. Other sets follow, including, "Circles of Destruction," "Trap Boxing," "Counterattacks," and "Foot Angles."

At a more advanced level, Wei Kuen Do practitioners learn such things as the use of shoulder rolls, parries, deflections and cross-redirections in free fighting. But progression in this art is non-linear in the sense that the student is not required to master one technique before moving on to the next. For example, deflections feature in the tenth form in the Angles of Attack, and glimpses of other, more advanced techniques frequently appear in forms that come "prior" to the point at which the syllabus explicitly focuses on those particular moves.

The physical aspects of the practice of Wei Kuen Do are complemented—and sometimes even superseded—by its mental and spiritual dimensions. As students work their way through the technical requirements of this art, it is understood that they are constantly seeking to integrate the tools of their art and to advance the level of their understanding and appreciation, from the first stage of simply developing those tools, to refining, dissolving and ultimately expressing those same instruments in both their martial arts as well as in their everyday lives.

滙拳道
用拳猛击 勾拳 抄拳 砸拳 斧手 反擘拳
勾踢 扫腿 側踢 正踢
十角度進攻 全面摧毀 擒拿 反击 步法
捲背 格擋 将勁 迎击
創制 粹煉 融會 無形

THE WEI KUEN DO SYLLABUS

滙拳道

XIII. ALWAYS STRIVING, NEVER ARRIVING...

Even after Master Fong had formulated the recipe for the art of Wei Kuen Do, he continued to add ingredients into the mix as he encounter new and effective fighting methods in his travels. His affiliation with Wally Jay, Remy Presas and George Dillman continued to inform his training and teaching methods throughout time they spent together on the seminar circuit in the 1980s and beyond. The pivotal roles of Jujitsu and Arnis in the Wei Kuen Do system have already been addressed, but anyone who has trained with Master Fong knows that if these arts are part of the "delivery system," then pressure points are "the targets." In this regard Leo credits Grandmaster George Dillman. Dillman—the only other surviving member of the original alliance of headmasters—remembers that special time:

GRANDMASTERS GEORGE DILLMAN AND LEO FONG

LEO THE LION-HEART

It was a different time in martial arts history—I am so glad it was my time... There were not many schools in the United States. Everybody seemed to know everyone teaching and they would all help each other. It was a time of introductions. Harry Smith was my main teacher and good friend to this very day. I was in the military and got transferred to Washington D.C. with a military police battalion. The martial arts were my true love. I went to train with Jhoon Rhee to learn how to kick better. I read a story in the newspaper about a Daniel K. Pai teaching in Virginia, very close to D.C., and went to meet him. Meeting master Pai opened up the world of many more great friendships: Danny Pai introduced me to Ed Parker. Ed Parker introduced me to Bruce Lee. And Bruce Lee introduced me to Wally Jay and Leo Fong.

Anytime you were with other martial artists, you shared knowledge and naturally talked of other martial arts greats. Bruce Lee, Daniel Pai and I were talking over Chinese food one day and Bruce asked me, "Who are some of the best on the East Coast?" I said, "There are many." He leaned in and said, "Which one would you think twice about fighting in a real situation?" I thought hard and then gave him a couple names. I then posed the same question to Bruce. He said, "There are a couple of really tough people teaching in California especially Ed Parker, Wally Jay and Leo Fong. They are no nonsense, get on the mat and prove yourself guys." I asked what he meant by that, and he said, "If you ask Professor Jay a question, he does not give you an answer—he gets you on the mat and demonstrates his answer on you! Leo Fong teaches Chinese boxing style. He is really fast and hits very hard. You must meet these two and train with them."

After Bruce Lee passed away I remembered his words. I traveled to Canada to meet and train with Professor Jay. I went to a tournament in Atlantic City to meet Leo Fong. Leo and I hit it off immediately, I think because of the Bruce Lee connection. Wally Jay and I went on a world tour, teaching and sharing seminars in some 30 different countries. Leo Fong and I grew close through bringing him to my school to teach and getting many members of my association to bring him in. Leo has so much to teach and share. He is like an encyclopedia of martial arts and the fighting game in general. Leo Fong trains like no other. I always tell people, "When you bring him in for a seminar, expect the best training session of your life." Leo has always worked out as if he had a pro-fight coming up next week!

Leo Fong and I are 15 years apart in age, but have had similar fighting careers. I started as a boxer, before I did karate. So did Leo. When I read about his boxing career I was so glad that I did not have to meet him in the ring! He would cut people down with those fast hands, like a lumber jack taking down a tree... I truly admire, respect and love him and his family. He is a teacher of teachers; a master among masters. —George Dillman

GRANDMASTERS CHARLES TERRY, LEO FONG, GEORGE DILLMAN AND WALLY JAY

During the 1980s, a decade that epitomized selfishness in many ways, something truly remarkable happened in the North American martial arts community. In the midst of fierce competition among the various martial styles, schools and organizations, a group of grandmasters—all recognized experts and innovators in their particular disciplines—banded together to share ideas, techniques and seminars with each other. The result was that their students the world over enjoyed a breadth and depth of instruction unparalleled in common experience. The ancient fighting arts of Japan, China, Okinawa and the Philippines blended together in a chorus that preserved the distinctiveness of each voice but combined to produce a four-part harmony the strength of which truly exceeded the sum of its parts. —"Remy Presas Remembered," *Journal of Asian Martial Arts*, 2007.

WEI KUEN DO PRINCIPLE: ALWAYS STRIVING, NEVER ARRIVING...

WEI KUEN DO

漢拳道

XIV. THE TOOLS

> *When asked what he would do if he was given four hours to chop down a tree, Abraham Lincoln said that he would spend the first three hours sharpening his axe.* —GMLF

Presented in this chapter are the fundamental techniques of Wei Kuen Do. This is not to suggest that no other techniques are permitted, taught or indeed of value under appropriate circumstances in this system of self-defense. Rather, these are simply the principal tools of the Wei Kuen Do practitioner; the techniques that must be drilled to the point that their execution becomes second nature.

WEI KUEN DO

HAND TECHNIQUES

The essential hand-weapon of the Wei Kuen Do practitioner is the fist. In contrast to certain "harder" styles of martial arts, the WKD fist is closed but relaxed (except on impact with a hard target). The feeling of this fist-form helps the student to cultivate the relaxed focus and lightning speed that is the trademark of WKD handwork.

☯ **The Forward Punch—Jab and Straight/Cross**: In developing combinations of punches it may be analytically helpful to consider the three dimensions of the Cartesian coordinate system: The x-axis represents side to side motion. The y-axis deals with up and down movement. And the z-axis covers the forward and backward plane; the dimension in which the straight punch travels. The straight punch (sometimes called a "cross") travels in a direct path from the practitioner toward the opponent along the aforementioned z-axis. When delivered with the lead hand using a snapping motion, it is a jab. When launched from the rear hip with greater power it is a straight, also known as a cross or a reverse punch depending on the system and the particular application.

☯ **The Hook:** A good hook's trajectory initially travels more-or-less along the z-axis and then snaps in sharply from the side, more in line with the x-axis, so as to strike from the side without telegraphing its intended destination. When striking the side of the chin—perhaps the most attractive target— it twists the head sideways violently, often resulting in a knock out.

☯ **The Uppercut:** This strike moves primarily along the y-axis, rising up to lift the target, whether it be the underside of the ribs, the kidneys or the chin. This punch derives much of its power from the hips and legs, and can quite literally lift the opponent off his feet.

☯ **The Backfist**: A favored Choy Lay Fut strike, the backfist strikes with the large, flat surface of the back of the hand and develops much of its power from the ballistic, spinning method with which it is commonly delivered. Often launched by rotating the body in a full circle, this technique harnesses the muscles of the legs and torso in an uncoiling motion, and its "flight path" is primarily along the x-axis.

☯ **The Hammerfist:** A staple of the Sil Lum style, the hammerfist is one of the most powerful hand weapons available to any martial artist, making its impact with the tightly coiled little finger side of the clenched fist, and usually crossing the *opponent's* centerline and returning in order to strike its target. The trajectory of this technique is typically along the x-axis (or the y-axis if delivered in a descending path). In order to appreciate the power of the hammerfist, ask yourself if you had to break a half dozen boards balanced between two cinder blocks, which hand technique would pose the least risk to the fragile bones of the hand.

☯ **The Axefist:** The axefist is simply a variation of the hammerfist. It employs the same hand shape and striking surface as the hammerfist but describes a striking method in which the blow is delivered with the knuckles facing up instead of down (sometime referred to as an inverted hammerfist). One advantage to this variation is that the fist generally does not need to cross the centerline in order to strike its target.

☯ **Advanced Techniques:** Additional, advanced hand techniques are taught to Wei Kuen Do practitioners as they progress through the art's syllabus.

WEI KUEN DO

LEG TECHNIQUES

Wei Kuen Do leg strikes are typically, but not always, delivered below the waist. They use a variety of surfaces, including the ball, knife-edge, instep and arch, to strike a range of different targets. One key feature of WKD kicks is that they are integrated into strikes, defense and counterstrikes as part of various combinations rather than being viewed as separate techniques.

● **The Hooking Kick:** The Wei Kuen Do hook kick is typically delivered at an oblique angle using the instep and a favorite target is the inside (or outside) of the opponent's thigh. It is sometimes described as, "a low roundhouse kick."

● **The Sweeping Kick:** Moving along a diagonal path—either outside-to-in or inside-to-out)—and often striking with the arch of the foot, this kick's primary purpose is to sweep the opponent's leg out from under him, or at least injure the target limb, thereby impairing its function as both a striking weapon and part of a stable base. This technique is sometimes called, "a step-over kick."

WEI KUEN DO

● **The Side Kick:** Delivered in a straight line using the knife edge of the foot, this low kick can easily buckle or dislocate the knee if delivered from the back or side, and can also be used to strike painful pressure points in a variety of location below the waist.

● **The Front Kick:** The front kick also travels in a straight line and typically strikes with the ball of the foot, although the heel and even the toes or instep may be used under certain circumstances.

GRANDMASTERS CHARLES TERRY AND LEO FONG

FOOTWORK

Wei Kuen Do footwork has a light, sliding, agile feel to it. The goal is to move quickly and smoothly in and around striking distance without telegraphing intent, and to ensure that an oblique body angle is presented to the opponent at all times.

● **The V-Step:** The fundamental footwork technique in Wei Kuen Do is the V-step, so named because the practitioner's feet trace the letter "V" on the floor as the move is performed. In a left foot forward fighting stance, for example, the lead foot is placed at the "top" of the left "arm" of the notional letter "V." When the practitioner decides to reorient to a right foot forward stance, he slides his rear/right foot forward so that it now rests at the "top" of the right "arm" of the letter "V," and slides the left foot back to the vertex of the notional letter. In so doing, the angle of his body will shift accordingly, like a swinging door. The feeling—and often the very purpose—of this move is avoiding a frontal attack.

● **Milling on the Retreat:** While instinct and the laws of physics support the idea that it is easier to deliver a powerful blow from a stable, advancing, or rising base, the practitioner of WKD must also learn to strike while stepping backwards or dropping down. It is an unusual sensation at first, but, like many other things, a valuable skill that can be acquired with patience and practice. This move features prominently, for example, at the conclusion of most of the Angle of Attack forms.

WEI KUEN DO

DEFENSIVE TECHNIQUES

As Wei Kuen Do senior master Adam James often says, the fundamental concept underpinning the art's defensive measures is that, "four ounces of pressure defeats four thousand pounds of force." Accordingly, the progression of the following techniques represents a spectrum of employing less and less force to defeat the incoming attack.

☯ **Shoulder Roll:** One of the most important lessons in self-defense is to use the least effort required to avoid getting hit. Muhammad Ali, for example, was skilled at ducking strikes with minimal movement or pulling his head back just far enough to avoid taking the brunt of an incoming blow. In Wei Kuen Do, the student learns to "shrug" the shoulder on the side of an incoming hook punch, tucking the chin and covering the face with the opposite palm so as to avoid getting hit without having to make an expansive blocking motion. This technique, famously employed by Floyd Mayweather, is known in WKD as, "a shoulder roll."

☯ **Parry:** By now the vast majority of the martial arts world has accepted the fact that the clenched-fist, cross-body, wide-sweeping hand techniques seen in many classical forms are not in fact blocks despite the fact that they were taught and practiced as such for decades in the West. Rather, anyone who has the slightest experience sparring recognizes that a far faster and more efficient way to prevent the opponent's strike from reaching its intended target is to knock it off course with a quick, open-hand, slapping parry. The Wei Kuen Do parry is performed with a light touch, "Like a fly landing on your arm."

☯ **Deflection:** If a shoulder roll may be said to prevent an incoming strike from reaching its target at the destination of its course, and a parry knocks the opponent's strike off course before impact, then a deflection prevents the strike from truly getting on course in the first place. In WKD, deflection can refer to physical diversion of a technique but also the tactical, strategic and even philosophical avoidance of a clash. By deflecting in conjunction with defusing and detaching ("the three Ds" of WKD) practitioners learn to control their physical proximity to the opponent while simultaneously managing the mental and emotional aspects of combat, thereby controlling the fight and its outcome, or indeed whether there is a fight at all...

☯ **Cross Redirection:** Wei Kuen Do practitioners learn to throw a cross and then redirect their follow-up strike based on the opponent's initial reaction. For example, many, if not most, trained fighters will block a cross with an inward parry. The student of Wei Kuen Do recognizes this defense and redirect his cross to, say, a hook punch. This fourth level represents the practice of WKD at its highest level since the student is not merely blocking, parrying or deflecting an existing attack, but is rather inviting a reaction from the opponent and then tailoring the response to take advantage of that reaction.

The secret to mastering these fundamentals is surprisingly simple in concept but extremely difficult in execution: Practice, practice, practice. And when you think you are done, practice some more…

XV. THE TEN ANGLES OF ATTACK

The proposition that the martial arts should begin and end with respect has been attributed to many masters over the centuries, perhaps most notably, Gichin Funakoshi, the acknowledged father of modern karate. Whatever the source of this wise teaching, it is a fundamental tenet of Wei Kuen Do as well, and manifests itself in many ways, including the performance of a show of respect at the outset and conclusion of training.

COURTESY

Combining this traditional courtesy with WKD's no nonsense approach to combat, the practitioner executes a simple bow from the waist and then drops immediately into a fighting stance to commence practice.

滙拳道

MEDITATION

If the WKD practitioner intends to focus to a significant degree on the internal aspects of the set of techniques he is about to perform, he may also engage in some meditation or chi-building exercises beforehand. This typically involves taking a number of deep breaths after bowing but before beginning the form while focusing the mind and energy inward. This breathing exercise is usually accompanied—and indeed assisted—by elevating the open hands, fingers pointed upward, on the inhale, and lowering them with the fingers pointed downward on the exhale.

There is far more to the process than the rudimentary physical aspects described above, but this brief explanation should serve to orient the student sufficiently to the concept before beginning in-person training with a WKD instructor.

THE TEN ANGLES OF ATTACK

At a fundamental level, the Angles of Attack catalogue, showcase and hone the primary, offensive hand-weapons of the system. They are comprised of jabs, straights, hooks, uppercuts, hammerfists, axefists, traps and parries, deployed in combination and executed using both the left and right hands. It is important to note that while the Angles of Attack emphasize offense, they truly form the foundation of Wei Kuen Do; not just the offensive techniques. Dedicated practice of the Angles of Attack will serve to develop, refine, dissolve and ultimately express the tools of the Wei Kuen Do practitioner. They can be broken down and explored in detail as an offensive set, a defensive/counter set, a set for feinting and faking, and so on. The Angles of Attack are designed to be the perfect tools with which to plumb the depths of the Wei Kuen Do system.

The first pattern in the Angles of Attack provides a kind of "inventory" of the fundamental fist weapons. It is presented frame-by-frame below in order to acclimatize the student to this presentation format. The photographic depiction of the remaining forms in this set is somewhat more compressed.

❂ **Practice Pointer:** While most the majority of the Wei Kuen Do forms are intended for "dual execution"—that is, mirror image practice on both the left and right sides—from the outset, the Angles of Attack are initially practiced unilaterally. It is only at more advanced levels, when executed as counters, fakes, and other types of variations, that bilateral execution is employed.

Angles of Attack, Form One: "Inventory of Techniques"

1. From a left foot forward fighting stance, execute a left jab.

2. V-step to a right foot forward stance and execute a right cross.

3. V-step to a left foot forward stance and execute a left hook.

4. V-STEP TO RIGHT FOOT FORWARD AND EXECUTE RIGHT UPPERCUT.

5. WITHOUT CHANGING STANCE, EXECUTE RIGHT HOOK (OFF THE UPPERCUT).

6. V-STEP TO LEFT FOOT FORWARD STANCE AND EXECUTE LEFT UPPERCUT.

7. WITHOUT CHANGING STANCE, EXECUTE LEFT HOOK (OFF THE UPPERCUT).

8. V-STEP TO RIGHT FOOT FORWARD, RIGHT HAMMERFIST (LEFT TO RIGHT).

9. V-STEP TO LEFT FOOT FORWARD, LEFT HAMMERFIST (RIGHT TO LEFT).

10. V-STEP TO RIGHT FOOT FORWARD, RIGHT AXEFIST (RIGHT TO LEFT).

11. V-STEP TO LEFT FOOT FORWARD, LEFT AXEFIST (LEFT TO RIGHT).

◉ **Practice Pointer:** This first form consists of an unusually high number of paired techniques (e.g. left hammer, right hammer; left axe, right axe). Accordingly, it is perhaps most easily conceptualized as an "inventory" of the fundamental hand techniques employed by the WKD practitioner.

◉ **Practice Pointer:** As with many aspects of Wei Kuen Do, variations are not only permitted; they are encouraged. Accordingly, the axefist may also be performed as a knifehand (shuto) depending on the practitioner's preference.

Notes: _____

_____

_____

ANGLES OF ATTACK, FORM TWO: "CLEARING THE SHELF" (RIGHT)

1. BEGIN IN LEFT FOOT FORWARD STANCE; LEFT JAB, HOOK-OFF-JAB.
2. REMAIN LEFT FOOT FORWARD (NO STEP); RIGHT CROSS TO THE BODY.
3. V-STEP TO RIGHT FOOT FORWARD; RIGHT UPPERCUT.
4. REMAIN RIGHT FOOT FORWARD (NO STEP); LEFT HOOK.
5. V-STEP TO LEFT FOOT FORWARD; (RETREATING) RIGHT CROSS.

● Practice Pointer: The right uppercut lifts the opponent's head as though putting it up on a shelf, and the left hook clears it off the shelf.

● Practice Pointer: While not shown in the photo sequence above, the Grandmaster often adds a hook-off-the-jab following the initial move. Always striving, never arriving…

Notes: _____

_____

_____

_____

_____

_____

WEI KUEN DO

ANGLES OF ATTACK, FORM THREE: "CLEARING THE SHELF" (LEFT)

1. BEGIN IN LEFT FOOT FORWARD STANCE; LEFT JAB, HOOK-OFF-JAB.
2. REMAIN LEFT FOOT FORWARD (NO STEP); RIGHT CROSS TO BODY.
3. V-STEP TO RIGHT FOOT FORWARD; RIGHT HOOK.
4. REMAIN RIGHT FOOT FORWARD; LEFT UPPERCUT.
5. REMAIN RIGHT FOOT FORWARD; LEFT HOOK.
6. V-STEP TO LEFT FOOT FORWARD; (RETREATING) STRAIGHT RIGHT.

☯ **Practice Pointer:** This time the right hook moves the opponent's head to the left, where the left uppercut "lifts" it as though putting it up on a shelf, and the left hook "clears it off the shelf" again.

☯ **Practice Pointer:** While not shown in the photo sequence above, the Grandmaster often adds a hook-off-the-jab following the initial move. Always striving, never arriving…

Notes: _____

_____

_____

_____

_____

_____

_____

_____

Angles of Attack, Form Four: "Double Left Hooks"

1. Begin left foot forward; left jab.
2. V-step to right foot forward; right cross.
3. Remain right foot forward; left hook.
4. Remain right foot forward; right uppercut.
5. Remain right foot forward; left hook.
6. V-step to left foot forward; (retreating) right cross.

L JAB   R CROSS   L HOOK   R UPPERCUT   L HOOK   R CROSS

☯ **Practice Pointer:** The "left jab—right cross—left hook" combination is arguably the best knockout technique in all of boxing. The left jab distracts and sets the combination up; the right cross causes a fair bit of consternation all by itself; and the smoking left hook finishes the job every time. WKD's fourth form picks up on the power of this combination, and throws in an extra left hook, just for good measure...

Notes: _____

_____

_____

_____

_____

_____

_____

WEI KUEN DO

ANGLES OF ATTACK, FORM FIVE: "LEFT TRAP"

1. BEGIN LEFT FOOT FORWARD; LEFT JAB, HOOK-OFF-JAB.
2. REMAIN LEFT FOOT FORWARD; RIGHT CROSS TO BODY.
3. V-STEP TO RIGHT FOOT FORWARD; LEFT TRAP; RIGHT BACKFIST.
4. REMAIN RIGHT FOOT FORWARD; LEFT HOOK.
5. REMAIN RIGHT FOOT FORWARD; RIGHT UPPERCUT;
6. REMAIN RIGHT FOOT FORWARD; LEFT HOOK.
7. V-STEP TO LEFT FOOT FORWARD; (RETREATING) RIGHT CROSS.

☯ **Practice Pointer:** Most of the techniques in the fifth form should be familiar by now. The new additions are the trap (executed in this case by parrying the opponent's strike downward with the left hand right after the student's own low right cross) and the backfist (executed in this case by "rolling" the right fist up and forward from behind the left parry and striking over top).

☯ **Practice Pointer:** While not shown in the photo sequence above, the Grandmaster often adds a hook-off-the-jab following the initial move. Always striving, never arriving…

Notes: _____

_____

_____

_____

_____

_____

Angles of Attack, Form Six: "Right/Left Trap"

1. Begin left foot forward; left jab.

2. Remain left foot forward; left cross to body

3. Remain left foot forward; right trap; left backfist.

4. V-step to right foot forward; left trap; right backfist.

5. Remain right foot forward; left hook.

6. Remain right foot forward; right uppercut.

7. Remain right foot forward; left hook.

8. V-step to left foot forward; (retreating) right cross.

☻ **Practice Pointer:** As in the fifth form, this sixth form continues to train the student in trapping (executed in this case by parrying the opponent's strike downward with the right hand right after the student's own low left cross, striking over top of the parry with the left backfist, then reversing this procedure with a left parry/right backfist combination). It is helpful to note that there is no step on the first trap/backfist combination but there is on the second.

Notes: _____

_____

_____

_____

_____

WEI KUEN DO

ANGLES OF ATTACK, FORM SEVEN: "STRIKE ON THREE PLANES"

1. BEGIN LEFT FOOT FORWARD; LEFT JAB.

2. V-STEP TO RIGHT FOOT FORWARD; RIGHT CROSS.

3. REMAIN RIGHT FOOT FORWARD; LEFT UPPERCUT.

4. V-STEP TO LEFT FOOT FORWARD; LEFT HOOK.

5. REMAIN LEFT FOOT FORWARD; LOW RIGHT CROSS.

6. V-STEP TO RIGHT FOOT FORWARD; RIGHT UPPERCUT.

7. REMAIN RIGHT FOOT FORWARD; LEFT HOOK.

8. V-STEP TO LEFT FOOT FORWARD; (RETREATING) RIGHT CROSS.

◉ **Practice Pointer:** Some students find it helpful to conceptualize this form as four "pairs" of techniques. This form has the practitioner attacking in all dimensions:

Moves 1, 2, 5 and 8 move along the z-axis (here, moving forward);
Moves 3 and 6 travel the y-axis (here, moving upward);
Moves 4 and 7 track the x-axis (here moving left-to-right).

Notes: _____

_____

_____

_____

_____

_____

ANGLES OF ATTACK, FORM EIGHT: "STEPPING OFF CENTERLINE"

1. BEGIN LEFT FOOT FORWARD; LEFT JAB.

2. REMAIN LEFT FOOT FORWARD; LOW LEFT JAB.

3. REMAIN LEFT FOOT FORWARD; LEFT JAB.

4. SIDESTEP WITH RIGHT FOOT OFF CENTER LINE; RIGHT BODY HOOK.

5. RIGHT FOOT FORWARD; RIGHT UPPERCUT.

6. REMAIN RIGHT FOOT FORWARD; LEFT HOOK.

7. V-STEP TO LEFT FOOT FORWARD; (RETREATING) RIGHT CROSS.

● **Practice Pointer:** Now that the practitioner has started to become familiar with striking angles in the context of so-called "stand up fighting," this form expands the concept by increasing the focus on body angling.

Notes: _____

_____

_____

_____

_____

_____

_____

WEI KUEN DO

ANGLES OF ATTACK, FORM NINE: "LEFT SIDE EXERCISE"

1. BEGIN LEFT FOOT FORWARD; LEFT JAB.

2. REMAIN LEFT FOOT FORWARD; LEFT HOOK.

3. REMAIN LEFT FOOT FORWARD; LEFT UPPERCUT.

4. REMAIN LEFT FOOT FORWARD; LEFT HOOK.

5. REMAIN LEFT FOOT FORWARD; LEFT HAMMERFIST.

6. REMAIN LEFT FOOT FORWARD; LEFT AXEFIST.

7. V-STEP TO RIGHT FOOT FORWARD; LOW RIGHT CROSS.

8. REMAIN RIGHT FOOT FORWARD; RIGHT UPPERCUT.

9. REMAIN RIGHT FOOT FORWARD; LEFT HOOK.

10. V-STEP TO LEFT FOOT FORWARD; (RETREATING) RIGHT CROSS.

☯ **Practice Pointer:** While this form focuses on the use of the left hand, like all the other Angles of Attack, it can and should be practiced on the other (right) side as well.

Notes: _____

_____

_____

_____

_____

汇拳道

ANGLES OF ATTACK, FORM TEN: "SIDE SLIPPING"

1. BEGIN LEFT FOOT FORWARD; PARRY/"SLIP" LEFT.

2. REMAIN LEFT FOOT FORWARD; LEFT UPPERCUT TO BODY.

3. REMAIN LEFT FOOT FORWARD; RIGHT HOOK.

4. REMAIN LEFT FOOT FORWARD; LEFT HOOK.

5. V-STEP TO RIGHT FOOT FORWARD; PARRY/"SLIP" RIGHT.

6. REMAIN RIGHT FOOT FORWARD; RIGHT UPPERCUT TO BODY.

7. REMAIN RIGHT FOOT FORWARD; LEFT HOOK.

8. REMAIN RIGHT FOOT FORWARD; RIGHT HOOK.

[CLOSING MOVE TO TEN ANGLES OF ATTACK FORM]

9. FEET PARALLEL, ELEVATE AND LOWER FISTS WITH DEEP BREATH.

● **Practice Pointer:** The new technique here is, "the slip." In essence, the practitioner sidesteps the incoming strike and guards the head with the open, "inside" hand (in the first, second and third picture above, the right hand). But it should be noted that the, "outside" hand (in the first, second and third picture above, the left hand) may help to deflect the incoming strike along the way.

Notes: _____

_____

_____

XVI. CIRCLES OF DESTRUCTION

The Circles of Destruction are performed in response to a variety of attacks, launched from various quarters. Unlike the Angles of Attack, the Circles of Destruction are triggered by the opponent first initiating an attack. They also differ from the Angles of Attack in that they are "dual execution" patterns, meaning that they are meant to be practiced to both the left and right sides, as mirror images of each other. While the Circles of Destruction are catalytically defensive, their offensive effectiveness is undeniable.

☯ **Practice Pointer:** The power of the Circles of Destruction is grounded in the overwhelming effectiveness of cycling a series of different strikes along the same circular trajectory. The relative speed, variety and momentum of such an onslaught is truly devastating, and it is fully expected that the opponent will be neutralized long before all of the strikes in the sequence have been delivered. It is, however, infinitely preferable to the WKD practitioner for the opponent to run out of defenses before he himself runs out of attacks!

☯ **Practice Pointer:** Virtually every WKD form can be practiced to the left or right side. This principle is explicitly articulated in the Circles of Destruction, which are sometimes numbered, "1A, 1B, 2A, 2B..." in order to distinguish between left and right side execution of each form.

☯ **Practice Pointer:** As in many arts, the preliminary and concluding techniques of many WKD forms are similar. They often begin with one or more straight punches to soften up, feel out and set up the opponent, and they typically conclude the same way as the practitioner re-opens the interval between himself and the opponent. Consistent with fundamental WKD philosophy, the number and variety of these opening and closing techniques is not strictly prescribed, and the student is encouraged to, "go with the flow," of the particular opponent and engagement. For the sake of consistency, however, a specific number and type is provided as a recommended "standard approach" herein.

WEI KUEN DO

CIRCLES OF DESTRUCTION, FORM ONE: "WINDMILL/BACKFIST"

1. BEGIN LEFT FOOT FORWARD; SHIFT TO LEFT 45°; LEFT SWEEP BLOCK.

2. REMAIN LEFT FOOT FORWARD; RIGHT OUTWARD BLOCK

3. REMAIN LEFT FOOT FORWARD; LEFT "TAP" (TO CONTROL, NOT INJURE).

4. V-STEP TO RIGHT FOOT FORWARD; RIGHT BACKFIST (TO HEAD).

5. V-STEP TO LEFT FOOT FORWARD; LEFT HOOK (HEAD).

6. V-STEP TO RIGHT FOOT FORWARD; RIGHT UPPERCUT.

7. REMAIN RIGHT FOOT FORWARD; RIGHT HOOK.

8. V-STEP TO LEFT FOOT FORWARD; LEFT UPPERCUT.

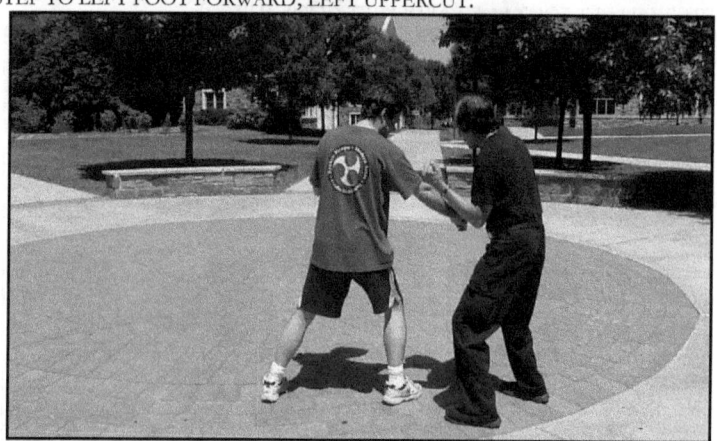

9. REMAIN LEFT FOOT FORWARD; LEFT HOOK.

10. REMAIN LEFT FOOT FORWARD; RIGHT CROSS [LEFT CROSS].

🟢 **Practice Pointer:** "Windmill block," is a convenient shorthand for the two-step defensive technique portrayed in pictures one and two. In this bifurcated technique, the outside hand sweeps inward to begin the parry, the motion of which is then taken over by the inside hand, which begins its trajectory at the outside hand's elbow and moves in an upward and outward direction from that point. The effect of this move is to allow the inside hand—sometimes called "the hidden hand"—to take over the parry in a surprising manner while freeing up the outside hand to launch a counterattack.

🟢 **Practice Pointer:** The WKD "tap," portrayed in the third picture can also be considered a part or variation of the windmill block's deflecting/controlling technique, thereby making it a, "three-step" technique.

Notes: _____

_____

_____

_____

_____

_____

_____

CIRCLES OF DESTRUCTION, FORM TWO: "ROLL/LADDER/BACKFIST"

1. BEGIN LEFT FOOT FORWARD; LEFT SHOULDER ROLL (RIGHT HAND COVER).

2. REMAIN LEFT FOOT FORWARD; LEFT OUTWARD TAP/BLOCK.

3. V-STEP TO RIGHT FOOT FORWARD; RIGHT TAP/BLOCK.

4. Remain right foot forward; left tap/block.

5. Remain right foot forward; right backfist.

6. V-step to left foot forward; left hook.

7-12. V-STEP TO RIGHT FOOT FORWARD; RIGHT UPPERCUT; RIGHT HOOK; V-STEP TO LEFT FOOT FORWARD; LEFT UPPERCUT; LEFT HOOK; RIGHT CROSS [LEFT CROSS].

❂ **Practice Pointer:** Each of the Circles of Destruction—and many other Wei Kuen Do forms as well—have three distinct stages; a beginning, a middle and an end, so to speak.

1. The opening gambit is the initial defense from the opponent's attack; an outside parry in Circle One and a shoulder roll in Circle Two.

2. The middle of the action is the primary counter-attack; a backfist/hook combination in both Circles One and Two, ideally intended to finish the fight.

3. The endgame consists of a combination of follow-on techniques that may not be needed if the middle moves have had the intended effect, but are prescribed and practiced nonetheless so as to ensure that the practitioner's attacks outlast the opponent's defenses.

❂ **Practice Pointer:** Almost every one of the Circles of Destruction forms employs the same, or a very similar, finishing combination (uppercut, hook, uppercut, hook, cross [cross]). This pattern is illustrated frame-by-frame in Circle One, but abbreviated thereafter as a unified, serialized image.

Notes: _____

_____

_____

_____

_____

_____

_____

_____

CIRCLES OF DESTRUCTION, FORM THREE: "ROLL/HIT/BACKFIST"

1. BEGIN LEFT FOOT FORWARD; LEFT SHOULDER ROLL (RIGHT HAND COVER).

2. REMAIN LEFT FOOT FORWARD; LEFT OUTWARD TAP/BLOCK.

3. REMAIN LEFT FOOT FORWARD; RIGHT CROSS TO THE BODY.

4. REMAIN LEFT FOOT FORWARD; LEFT TRAP.†

5. V-STEP TO RIGHT FOOT FORWARD; RIGHT BACKFIST.

6. V-STEP TO LEFT FOOT FORWARD; LEFT HOOK.

7-12. V-STEP TO RIGHT FOOT FORWARD; RIGHT UPPERCUT; RIGHT HOOK; V-STEP TO LEFT FOOT FORWARD; LEFT UPPERCUT; LEFT HOOK; RIGHT CROSS [LEFT CROSS].

❂ **Practice Pointer:** The WKD practitioner continues refining the tools of his trade, he begins to move away from rote repetition and routine, and starts to develop the ability to "flow" with the form, and indeed, the fight. For example, the fourth move in this form traps the opponent's follow-up strike (in the sequence shown above, a straight right) allowing the WKD practitioner to deliver a backfist over the top of the trapped limb. If, however, the opponent counterstrikes with the opposite hand (in the sequence shown above, the *left* hand), WKD trapping principles dictate a different response. Each move has a corresponding counter, and the practitioner begins to feel which is required in any given situation.

† **Variation:** If the opponent counterstrikes with the opposite hand (in the sequence shown above, the left hand), the WKD practitioner simply sidesteps, covers and hooks off the body-cross, then taps down off the hook, and executes a backfist with the opposite hand, followed by the familiar, "hook, uppercut-hook, uppercut-hook, cross-cross," sequence to end the form.

Notes: _____

_____

_____

_____

_____

_____

_____

WEI KUEN DO

CIRCLES OF DESTRUCTION, FORM FOUR: "ROLL/DOUBLE BACKFIST"

1. BEGIN LEFT FOOT FORWARD; LEFT SHOULDER ROLL (RIGHT HAND COVER).

2. REMAIN LEFT FOOT FORWARD; LEFT OUTWARD TAP/BLOCK.

3. V-STEP TO RIGHT FOOT FORWARD; RIGHT TAP/BLOCK.

4. Remain right foot forward; left tap/block.

5. Remain right foot forward; Right backfist.

6. Remain right foot forward; Low left cross.

7. Remain right foot forward; Right trap.

8. V-step to left foot forward; Left backfist.

9. V-step to right foot forward; Right hook.

10-14. V-STEP TO LEFT FOOT FORWARD; LEFT UPPERCUT; LEFT HOOK; V-STEP TO RIGHT FOOT FORWARD; RIGHT UPPERCUT; RIGHT HOOK; LEFT CROSS [RIGHT CROSS].

☯ **Practice Pointer:** The now-familiar finishing combination in the Circles of Destruction (uppercut, hook, uppercut, hook, cross, cross) can be varied according to situation and taste, but, as with many practices—martial and otherwise—it is important to learn the rules before bending or breaking them.

Notes: _____

_____

_____

_____

_____

_____

_____

_____

_____

_____

_____

_____

_____

CIRCLES OF DESTRUCTION, FORM FIVE: PARRY KICK LEFT-TO-RIGHT

1. BEGIN LEFT FOOT FORWARD; LOW LEFT PARRY TO KICK (LEFT-TO-RIGHT).

2. REMAIN LEFT FOOT FORWARD; RIGHT OUTWARD PARRY TO PUNCH.

3. REMAIN LEFT FOOT FORWARD; LEFT TAP.

4. REMAIN RIGHT FOOT FORWARD; RIGHT BACKFIST.

5. V-STEP TO LEFT RIGHT FOOT FORWARD; LEFT HOOK.

6-12. V-STEP TO RIGHT FOOT FORWARD; RIGHT UPPERCUT; RIGHT HOOK; V-STEP TO LEFT FOOT FORWARD; LEFT UPPERCUT; LEFT HOOK; RIGHT CROSS [LEFT CROSS].

Notes: _____

◉ **Practice Pointer:** Between pictures two and three, Grandmaster Fong will often insert an uppercut.

Notes: _____

CIRCLES OF DESTRUCTION, FORM SIX: PARRY KICK RIGHT-TO-RIGHT

1. BEGIN LEFT FOOT FORWARD; LOW RIGHT PARRY TO KICK (RIGHT-TO-RIGHT).

2. REMAIN LEFT FOOT FORWARD; LEFT SWEEP BLOCK TO PUNCH.

3. REMAIN LEFT FOOT FORWARD; RIGHT PARRY.

4. Remain left foot forward; Left tap.

5. V-step to right foot forward; Right backfist.

5. V-step to left foot forward; Left hook.

7-11. V-STEP TO RIGHT FOOT FORWARD; RIGHT UPPERCUT; RIGHT HOOK; V-STEP TO LEFT FOOT FORWARD; LEFT UPPERCUT; LEFT HOOK; RIGHT CROSS [LEFT CROSS].

☯ **Practice Pointer:** Between pictures three and four, Grandmaster Fong will often insert an uppercut.

Notes: _____

WEI KUEN DO

CIRCLES OF DESTRUCTION, FORM SEVEN: PARRY KICK LEFT-TO-LEFT

1. BEGIN RIGHT FOOT FORWARD; LOW LEFT PARRY TO KICK (LEFT-TO-LEFT)

2. V-STEP TO LEFT FOOT FORWARD; RIGHT PARRY TO PUNCH.

3. REMAIN LEFT FOOT FORWARD; LEFT TAP.

4. V-STEP TO RIGHT FOOT FORWARD; RIGHT BACKFIST.

5. V-STEP TO LEFT FOOT FORWARD; LEFT HOOK.

6-10. V-STEP TO RIGHT FOOT FORWARD; RIGHT UPPERCUT; RIGHT HOOK; V-STEP TO LEFT FOOT FORWARD; LEFT UPPERCUT; LEFT HOOK; RIGHT CROSS [LEFT CROSS].

◉ **Practice Pointer:** Between pictures two and three, Grandmaster Fong will often insert an uppercut.

Notes: _____

WEI KUEN DO

CIRCLES OF DESTRUCTION, FORM EIGHT: SAME SIDE WRAP (PUNCH)

1. BEGIN RIGHT FOOT FORWARD; LEFT INSIDE PARRY.

2. REMAIN RIGHT FOOT FORWARD; RIGHT HAMMERFIST.

3. V-STEP TO LEFT FOOT FORWARD; RIGHT WRAP.

4. REMAIN LEFT FOOT FORWARD; LEFT HOOK.

5-9. V-STEP TO RIGHT FOOT FORWARD; RIGHT UPPERCUT; RIGHT HOOK; V-STEP TO LEFT FOOT FORWARD; LEFT UPPERCUT; LEFT HOOK; RIGHT CROSS [LEFT CROSS].

☯ **Practice Pointer:** By tying up the opponent's dominant hand, and doing so from the outside, the WKD practitioner minimizes the opponent's weapons while maximizing the power of his own finishing technique (here, the left hook).

Notes: _____

_____

_____

_____

_____

_____

_____

WEI KUEN DO

CIRCLES OF DESTRUCTION, FORM NINE: "THROW AWAY" BLOCK

1. BEGIN LEFT FOOT FORWARD; LEFT SWEEP BLOCK.

2. REMAIN LEFT FOOT FORWARD; RIGHT OUTWARD BLOCK.

3. REMAIN LEFT FOOT FORWARD; LEFT HOOK TO BODY.

4. Remain left foot forward; Right tap.

5. Remain left foot forward; Left tap.

6. V-step to right foot forward; Right backfist.

WEI KUEN DO

7. V-STEP TO LEFT FOOT FORWARD; LEFT HOOK.

8-12. V-STEP TO RIGHT FOOT FORWARD; RIGHT UPPERCUT; RIGHT HOOK; V-STEP TO LEFT FOOT FORWARD; LEFT UPPERCUT; LEFT HOOK; RIGHT CROSS [LEFT CROSS].

◉ **Practice Pointer:** The right block (image two) and the right "tap" (image four) should feel almost like two halves if the same moves, as though the right hand briefly blocks the path of the opponent's right arm and then throws it away and down.

Notes: _____

_____

_____

_____

_____

_____

CIRCLES OF DESTRUCTION, FORM TEN: ELBOW SPIN

1. BEGIN RIGHT FOOT FORWARD; LEFT INSIDE PARRY.

2. REMAIN RIGHT FOOT FORWARD; RIGHT HAMMERFIST TO HEAD.

3. REMAIN RIGHT FOOT FORWARD; RIGHT HAMMERFIST TO ELBOW.

4. V-STEP TO LEFT FOOT FORWARD; LEFT ARM PULLS/RIGHT CONTROLS TO LOCK.

5. REMAIN LEFT FOOT FORWARD; RIGHT HAMMERFIST TO HEAD.

† **Variation:** The essence of Wei Kuen Do is variation. Here, the Grandmaster chose to use the, "elbow-spin-to-lock," not the, "elbow-spin-to-takedown," variation. As a result, his left hand is tied up at the end of the form, and can't execute move six (the left backfist). Had he chosen to perform the takedown variation, his left hand would be free and could perform move six. In addition, in the takedown variation, the opponent would not be facing away from the practitioner. As a result, the practitioner can finish this form with the now-familiar, "uppercut-hook, uppercut-hook, cross-cross," combination.

† CIRCLES OF DESTRUCTION, FORM TEN: TAKEDOWN VARIATION

1-6. BEGIN RIGHT FOOT FORWARD; RIGHT HAMMERFIST TO HEAD; RIGHT HAMMERFIST TO ARM; TAKEDOWN; RIGHT BACKFIST; LEFT BACKFIST.

SIFU ADAM JAMES

7-11. V-STEP TO RIGHT FOOT FORWARD; RIGHT UPPERCUT; RIGHT HOOK; V-STEP.

Notes: _____
_____
_____
_____
_____
_____
_____
_____

XVII. TRAPPING COMBINATIONS

Wei Kuen Do trapping is based on Wing Chun and Western Boxing, but over many years, Master Fong refined, polished and simplified these techniques to work devastatingly well in the context of free fighting. At the highest level—as with most WKD technique—it is executed without thought or deliberation. When practiced in this way it is referred to as, "trapping without trapping."

> The concepts of trapping contained in the trap-boxing portion of the Wei Kuen Do curriculum are a perfect interpretation of the martial arts in general. Each of the traps in this sequence has the concept of yin and yang built into them. If the opponent moves in one direction, you counter and strike. If the opponent moves in the opposite direction, you counter the opposite way. With repetition your brain becomes hard wired to reacting in every direction, cutting out the need for conscious thought and sharpening reflexes. Also, with limited grabbing, trap-boxing allows you to flow with your partner and not worry about hands slipping and strength failing, since as you rely on parrying and head and body movement. The concepts Leo has devised are a great tool for more realistic sparring sessions and developing real world self-defense skills. —Grandmaster Shane Lear

Each of the trapping combinations begins with an offensive move intended to elicit a specific response from the opponent, thereby allowing the WKD practitioner to anticipate the counter, and then counter that counter the instant it is deployed. When executed properly this kind of "three-step" attack can appear almost magical in that it is as though the WKD practitioner is reading his opponent's mind and foretelling the future.

The Wei Kuen Do Trapping Combinations are delivered with one of five offensive entries and then adjusted according to the opponent's defensive response:

1. Left jab.
2. Left jab, left hook to head, right cross to body.
3. Left jab, stepping right cross.
4. Left jab to body.
5. Left jab, stepping right uppercut.

TRAPPING COMBINATIONS, FORM ONE, VERSION ONE

1-7. LEFT JAB; (OPPONENT BLOCKS WITH LEFT HAND) RIGHT TRAP WITH LEFT BACKFIST TO HEAD; RIGHT CROSS TO HEAD; LEFT UPPERCUT; LEFT HOOK TO HEAD; STEPPING RIGHT UPPERCUT; RIGHT HOOK TO HEAD.

TRAPPING COMBINATIONS, FORM ONE, VERSION TWO

1-8. LEFT JAB, (OPPONENT BLOCKS WITH RIGHT HAND); LEFT HOOK TO HEAD; LEFT TRAP/PULL DOWN WITH STEPPING RIGHT BACKFIST TO HEAD; LEFT CROSS TO HEAD; RIGHT UPPERCUT; RIGHT HOOK TO HEAD; STEPPING LEFT UPPERCUT; LEFT HOOK TO HEAD.

Notes: _____

WEI KUEN DO

TRAPPING COMBINATIONS, FORM TWO, VERSION ONE

1-10. LEFT JAB; (OPPONENT BLOCKS WITH LEFT HAND) RIGHT TRAP WITH LEFT BACKFIST TO HEAD; (OPPONENT BLOCKS WITH RIGHT HAND) RIGHT TRAP FROM UNDER THEN STEPPING LEFT SHOVEL PUNCH TO RIBS; LEFT TRAP WITH STEPPING RIGHT BACKFIST TO HEAD; LEFT CROSS TO HEAD; RIGHT UPPERCUT; RIGHT HOOK TO HEAD; STEPPING LEFT UPPERCUT; LEFT HOOK TO HEAD.

TRAPPING COMBINATIONS, FORM TWO, VERSION TWO

1-11. LEFT JAB; (OPPONENT BLOCKS WITH RIGHT HAND) LEFT HOOK TO HEAD; LEFT TRAP/PULL DOWN WITH STEPPING RIGHT BACKFIST TO HEAD; (OPPONENT BLOCKS WITH LEFT HAND) LEFT TRAP FROM UNDER THEN STEPPING RIGHT SHOVEL PUNCH TO RIBS; RIGHT TRAP WITH STEPPING LEFT BACKFIST TO HEAD; RIGHT HOOK.

Notes: _____

_____
_____
_____
_____
_____
_____

TRAPPING COMBINATIONS, FORM THREE, VERSION ONE

1-9. LEFT JAB; LEFT HOOK TO HEAD; RIGHT CROSS TO BODY; (OPPONENT BLOCKS DOWN WITH RIGHT HAND) LEFT TRAP WITH STEPPING RIGHT BACKFIST TO HEAD; LEFT CROSS TO HEAD; RIGHT UPPERCUT; RIGHT HOOK TO HEAD; STEPPING LEFT HOOK TO HEAD.

TRAPPING COMBINATIONS, FORM THREE, VERSION TWO

1-10. LEFT JAB; LEFT HOOK TO HEAD; RIGHT CROSS TO BODY; (OPPONENT BLOCKS DOWN WITH LEFT HAND) STEPPING RIGHT HOOK TO HEAD; STEPPING LEFT BACKFIST TO HEAD; RIGHT CROSS TO HEAD; LEFT UPPERCUT; LEFT HOOK TO HEAD; STEPPING RIGHT UPPERCUT; RIGHT HOOK TO HEAD.

Notes: _____
_____
_____
_____
_____
_____
_____

TRAPPING COMBINATIONS, FORM FOUR, VERSION ONE

1-12. LEFT JAB; LEFT HOOK TO HEAD; RIGHT CROSS TO BODY; (OPPONENT BLOCKS DOWN WITH RIGHT HAND) LEFT TRAP WITH STEPPING RIGHT BACKFIST TO HEAD; (OPPONENT BLOCKS WITH LEFT HAND) LEFT TRAP FROM UNDER THEN STEPPING RIGHT SHOVEL PUNCH TO RIBS; RIGHT TRAP WITH STEPPING LEFT BACKFIST TO HEAD; RIGHT CROSS; LEFT UPPERCUT; LEFT HOOK TO HEAD; STEPPING RIGHT UPPERCUT; RIGHT HOOK TO HEAD.

TRAPPING COMBINATIONS, FORM FOUR, VERSION TWO

1-13. LEFT JAB; LEFT HOOK TO HEAD; RIGHT CROSS TO BODY; (OPPONENT BLOCKS DOWN WITH LEFT HAND) STEPPING RIGHT HOOK TO HEAD; STEPPING LEFT BACKFIST TO HEAD; (OPPONENT BLOCKS WITH RIGHT HAND) RIGHT TRAP FROM UNDER THEN STEPPING LEFT SHOVEL PUNCH TO RIBS; LEFT TRAP WITH STEPPING RIGHT BACKFIST TO HEAD; LEFT CROSS TO HEAD; RIGHT UPPERCUT; RIGHT HOOK TO HEAD; STEPPING LEFT UPPERCUT; LEFT HOOK TO HEAD.

Notes: _____
_____
_____
_____
_____
_____
_____

TRAPPING COMBINATIONS, FORM FIVE, VERSION ONE

1-9. LEFT JAB; STEPPING RIGHT CROSS; (OPPONENT BLOCKS WITH RIGHT HAND) LEFT TRAP WITH RIGHT BACKFIST TO HEAD; LEFT CROSS TO HEAD; RIGHT UPPERCUT; RIGHT HOOK TO HEAD; STEPPING LEFT UPPERCUT; LEFT HOOK.

TRAPPING COMBINATIONS, FORM FIVE, VERSION TWO

1-10. LEFT JAB; STEPPING RIGHT CROSS; (OPPONENT BLOCKS WITH LEFT HAND) RIGHT HOOK TO HEAD; RIGHT TRAP/PULL DOWN WITH STEPPING LEFT BACKFIST TO HEAD; RIGHT CROSS TO HEAD; LEFT UPPERCUT; LEFT HOOK TO HEAD; STEPPING RIGHT UPPERCUT; RIGHT HOOK TO HEAD.

Notes: _____
_____
_____
_____
_____
_____
_____

WEI KUEN DO

TRAPPING COMBINATIONS, FORM SIX, VERSION ONE

1-11. LEFT JAB; STEPPING RIGHT CROSS; (OPPONENT BLOCKS WITH RIGHT HAND) LEFT TRAP WITH RIGHT BACKFIST TO HEAD; (OPPONENT BLOCKS WITH LEFT HAND) LEFT TRAP FROM UNDER THEN STEPPING RIGHT SHOVEL PUNCH TO RIBS; RIGHT TRAP WITH STEPPING LEFT BACKFIST TO HEAD; RIGHT CROSS TO HEAD; LEFT UPPERCUT; LEFT HOOK TO HEAD; STEPPING RIGHT UPPERCUT; RIGHT HOOK TO HEAD.

TRAPPING COMBINATIONS, FORM SIX, VERSION TWO

1-11. LEFT JAB; STEPPING RIGHT CROSS; (OPPONENT BLOCKS WITH LEFT HAND) RIGHT HOOK TO HEAD; RIGHT TRAP/PULL DOWN WITH STEPPING LEFT BACKFIST TO HEAD; (OPPONENT BLOCKS WITH RIGHT HAND) RIGHT TRAP FROM UNDER/STEPPING LEFT SHOVEL PUNCH TO RIBS; LEFT TRAP/STEPPING RIGHT BACKFIST TO HEAD; LEFT CROSS TO HEAD; RIGHT UPPERCUT; RIGHT HOOK TO HEAD; STEPPING LEFT UPPERCUT; LEFT HOOK TO HEAD.

Notes: _____
_____
_____
_____
_____
_____

TRAPPING COMBINATIONS, FORM SEVEN, VERSION ONE

1-8. LEFT JAB; LEFT JAB TO BODY; (OPPONENT BLOCKS WITH LEFT HAND) RIGHT TRAP WITH LEFT BACKFIST TO HEAD; RIGHT CROSS TO HEAD; LEFT UPPERCUT; LEFT HOOK TO HEAD; STEPPING RIGHT UPPERCUT; RIGHT HOOK TO HEAD.

TRAPPING COMBINATIONS, FORM SEVEN, VERSION TWO

1-9. LEFT JAB; LEFT JAB TO BODY; (OPPONENT BLOCKS WITH RIGHT HAND) LEFT HOOK TO HEAD; LEFT TRAP/PULL DOWN WITH STEPPING RIGHT BACKFIST TO HEAD; LEFT CROSS TO HEAD; RIGHT UPPERCUT; RIGHT HOOK TO HEAD; STEPPING LEFT UPPERCUT; LEFT HOOK TO HEAD.

Notes: _____

_____

_____

_____

_____

_____

_____

WEI KUEN DO

TRAPPING COMBINATIONS, FORM EIGHT, VERSION ONE

1-10. LEFT JAB; LEFT JAB TO BODY; (OPPONENT BLOCKS WITH LEFT HAND) RIGHT TRAP WITH LEFT BACKFIST TO HEAD; (OPPONENT BLOCKS WITH RIGHT HAND) RIGHT TRAP FROM UNDER THEN STEPPING LEFT SHOVEL PUNCH TO RIBS; LEFT TRAP WITH STEPPING RIGHT BACKFIST TO HEAD; LEFT CROSS TO HEAD; RIGHT UPPERCUT; RIGHT HOOK TO HEAD; STEPPING LEFT UPPERCUT; LEFT HOOK TO HEAD.

TRAPPING COMBINATIONS, FORM EIGHT, VERSION TWO

1-11. LEFT JAB; LEFT JAB TO BODY; (OPPONENT BLOCKS WITH RIGHT HAND) LEFT HOOK TO HEAD; LEFT TRAP/PULL DOWN WITH STEPPING RIGHT BACKFIST TO HEAD; (OPPONENT BLOCKS WITH LEFT HAND) LEFT TRAP FROM UNDER THEN STEPPING RIGHT SHOVEL PUNCH TO RIBS; RIGHT TRAP WITH STEPPING LEFT BACKFIST TO HEAD; RIGHT CROSS TO HEAD; LEFT UPPERCUT; LEFT HOOK TO HEAD; STEPPING RIGHT UPPERCUT; RIGHT HOOK TO HEAD.

Notes: _____
_____
_____
_____
_____
_____

匯拳道

TRAPPING COMBINATIONS, FORM NINE, VERSION ONE

1-8. LEFT JAB; STEPPING RIGHT UPPERCUT; (OPPONENT BLOCKS WITH RIGHT HAND) LEFT TRAP WITH RIGHT BACKFIST TO HEAD; LEFT CROSS TO HEAD; RIGHT UPPERCUT; RIGHT HOOK TO HEAD; STEPPING LEFT UPPERCUT; LEFT HOOK.

TRAPPING COMBINATIONS, FORM NINE, VERSION TWO

1-9. LEFT JAB; STEPPING RIGHT UPPERCUT; (OPPONENT BLOCKS WITH LEFT HAND) RIGHT HOOK TO HEAD; RIGHT TRAP/PULL DOWN WITH STEPPING LEFT BACKFIST TO HEAD; RIGHT CROSS TO HEAD; LEFT UPPERCUT; LEFT HOOK TO HEAD; STEPPING RIGHT UPPERCUT; RIGHT HOOK TO HEAD.

Notes: _____
_____
_____
_____
_____
_____
_____

WEI KUEN DO

TRAPPING COMBINATIONS, FORM TEN, VERSION ONE

1-10. LEFT JAB; STEPPING RIGHT UPPERCUT; (OPPONENT BLOCKS WITH RIGHT HAND) LEFT TRAP WITH RIGHT BACKFIST TO HEAD; (OPPONENT BLOCKS WITH LEFT HAND) LEFT TRAP FROM UNDER THEN STEPPING RIGHT SHOVEL PUNCH TO RIBS; RIGHT TRAP WITH STEPPING LEFT BACKFIST TO HEAD; RIGHT CROSS TO HEAD; LEFT UPPERCUT; LEFT HOOK TO HEAD; STEPPING RIGHT UPPERCUT; RIGHT HOOK TO HEAD.

TRAPPING COMBINATIONS, FORM TEN, VERSION TWO

1-11. LEFT JAB; STEPPING RIGHT UPPERCUT; (OPPONENT BLOCKS WITH LEFT HAND) RIGHT HOOK TO HEAD; RIGHT TRAP/PULL DOWN WITH STEPPING LEFT BACKFIST TO HEAD; (OPPONENT BLOCKS WITH RIGHT HAND) RIGHT TRAP FROM UNDER THEN STEPPING LEFT SHOVEL PUNCH TO RIBS; LEFT TRAP WITH STEPPING RIGHT BACKFIST TO HEAD; LEFT CROSS TO HEAD; RIGHT UPPERCUT; RIGHT HOOK TO HEAD; STEPPING LEFT UPPERCUT; LEFT HOOK TO HEAD.

Notes: _____

_____

_____

_____

XVIII. DEVELOP, REFINE, DISSOLVE, EXPRESS

Developing expertise in the art of Wei Kuen Do requires the practitioner to advance through four stages:

1. Developing the Tools—"Learn It": In this first stage, the student must learn to execute the techniques of the system properly. These include both the individual tools—like the hammerfist, the axefist and the side kick—as well as the combinations contained in the forms—like the Angles of Attack, the Circles of Destruction and the Trapping Combinations. In addition to those described in this book, there are many other individual and sets of techniques, including:

☯ **The Quick Counters:** These techniques are executed as counter-offensive moves deployed during the defense. They are intended to be fast and explosive, using the opponent's own offense against him.

☯ **The Footwork Counter Combinations:** These patterns were developed in recent years and, together with the Faking Combinations, are taught as advanced techniques only after students have worked through the Four Stages of Development with the Angles of Attack.

☯ **The Faking Combination:** These patterns were developed in recent years and, together with the Footwork Counter Combinations, are taught as advanced techniques only after students have worked through the Four Stages of Development with the Angles of Attack.

The emphasis in Wei Kuen Do is always on quality over quantity. In other words, it is not necessary for the student to "develop" every single tool before beginning to "refine," "dissolve" and "express" the tools.

WEI KUEN DO

WEI KUEN DO PRINCIPLE: PRACTICE ONE TECHNIQUE A THOUSAND TIMES RATHER THAN A THOUSAND TECHNIQUES ONLY ONCE.

    2. Refining the Tools—"Work It": At the second stage, the student strives to perfect the techniques and forms. This process requires much more than simply "knowing" them. For example, consider the difference between reciting the alphabet forwards and backwards. You know the order of the letters, and may therefore be able to provide them in reverse order, but the process will be halting and tentative. Saying—or indeed singing—the alphabet forwards by contrast, will be an relaxing and enjoyable task because it is so familiar. This ease of performance can only be achieved by repeated practice. There are no shortcuts.

    3. Dissolving the Tools—"Know It": At this level, the student begins to know deeply the techniques and forms of his art and "training wheels" are no longer required. His practice starts to grow beyond the confines of the pot in which it first sprouted, and he begins to experiment with variations and create new combinations using the tools he has now acquired.

    4. Expressing the Tools—"Live It": Once the student has truly internalized the techniques and patterns of Wei Kuen Do there is still one final stage of development to be achieved. In much the same way that a flowerpot shapes the soil it contains, the patterns and practices of Wei Kuen Do form the student's body and mind to the point that he (which term is intended to include both male and female practitioners) starts to move and think in accordance with its principles automatically. The pot can now fall away entirely and the sapling it once contained will continue to thrive. The art and the artist have now become one and the student practices Wei Kuen Do merely by moving through life and responding to stimuli instinctively. Those familiar with the Zen tale of the ox may find guidance in the eighth and ninth frames of the story.

滙拳道

IXX. ACRONYM, ANALOGY, ALLITERATION

5. THE FIVE "Fs"— FORM, FLOW, FOOTWORK, FEELING AND FREEDOM
4. THE FOUR ASPECTS—PHYSICAL, MENTAL, EMOTIONAL AND SPIRITUAL
3. THE THREE "Ds"—DEVELOPMENT, DISCIPLINE AND DISENGAGEMENT
2. THE DUALITY OF THE VOICE AND ECHO—CHI FUNG
1. ONENESS—"THE ZEN ZONE"

Like the late Master Lee, Master Fong is a believer in the value of mnemonic tools. Accordingly in their arts, acronyms, analogies and alliteration abound. These devices help the practitioner to appreciate training priorities, to absorb subtle ideas and to remember key points. In short, they help the student to refine, dissolve and express the tools he has learned. They act as waypoints along the path of the seeker. They supply the traveler with sustenance for the long journey. And they illuminate the trail on cloudy nights.

5. The Five "Fs"—Form, Flow, Footwork, Feeling, Freedom:

    i. Form: Form is the way you carry yourself. It is grace in movement. Good runners do not look jerky and uncoordinated. They must have form to achieve the best times. Bowlers must have good form before releasing the ball; otherwise the ball would roll into the gutter. In every sport an athlete must have grace and good form.

    ii. Flow: You must have fluidity of movement. If your techniques are choppy and without form, the opponent will easily counter. In the art of combat, the focus is on flow. When you execute a punch, you should instinctively feel the need to flow from one angle to the next without thinking. Every technique delivered should give the practitioner an emotional direction.

iii. Footwork: Footwork is not a separate component from Form and Flow; it is connected to the former two components. When emotional structure responds to an attack, footwork goes into play automatically. One way to develop a "hit without getting hit" mind-set is to perfect your footwork. No matter how deadly your techniques are, without proper footwork, your weapons will "wither on the vine."

iv. Feeling: Feeling or sensitivity is not confined to just physical contact; rather it is the emotional connection between you and your opponent. The moment your opponent moves on you, you instinctively know where he is. This will enable you to render his attack harmless or allow you to abort his attack with a counterattack before he can make his initial move.

v. Freedom: Learning the form and the footwork falls in the realm of developing the tools. The practitioner then refines these tools by striving for flow. The next step involves developing feel—not just for openings in the opponent's defense but also the presence of confidence and power within. At this stage the tools begin to dissolve. Finally, when the student no longer has to make a conscious effort to think about footwork, form, flow, and feeling, he will truly have achieved freedom of expression.

One of the keys to perfecting the Five Fs is awareness and consciousness as you repeat the various physical movements. The key to perfection is repetition. Repetition enables a practitioner to deepen the art. Far too many practitioners move from one technique to the next, skimming the surface but never plumbing the depths. In observing great fighters I have noticed one common denominator; the most effective techniques are the simple basic, moves practiced over and over for many years until they become rooted. It is only through years of repetitious practice that great fighters perfect the Five Fs.

4. The Four Aspects—Physical, Mental, Emotional, Spiritual:

i. Physical Aspect: The physical stage includes the development of the body. What a finely tuned racecar is to a driver, so is a well-conditioned body to a martial artist. During this phase of the training emphasis will be placed on Development of the Tools, such as body hardening, punches, kicks, throws, grappling as well as strength, agility, speed and stamina.

ii. Mental Aspect: Without mental discipline, all the technical skills in the world are useless. The ability to concentrate and focus on the job at hand will determine failure and success on combat. Emphasis at this stage will be placed on the development of awareness, stress training and Refining the Tools. Meditation is emphasized in order to develop a more relaxed posture in the midst of a stressful situation. Timing and speed are determined by mental response and awareness. When the practitioner is relaxed and able to concentrate, his reflexes are more responsive to his opponent's movements and he is able to intercept, dissolve and counter with ease.

iii. Emotional Aspect: Combat is the ability to express oneself through the physical tools. The ability to express is greatly influenced by the practitioner's emotional state. For instance, fear can be one of the most significant impediments to free expression. Fear can lead to shyness, over-aggressiveness, lack of confidence and many other character flaws. Total commitment to a technique is determined by how much confidence the practitioner has in himself and his ability. In this stage, the focus is on stress training, Refining the Tools and disharmonic emotional theory.

iv. Spiritual Aspect: When we speak of the spiritual stage, we are not speaking about religion necessarily. We are talking about a force that exists in the universe greater than man and machine. Harmonizing our life with this force adds strength to whatever we do. It adds meaning to our successes and wisdom to our failures. In essence, it is the source of power. In this stage the focus is on Dissolving the Tools.

3. The Three "Ds"—Development, Discipline, Disengagement:

The three "Ds" are the ingredients in the fuel that drives the process of truly learning the art of Wei Kuen Do. How they are achieved will vary according to the natural ability and ultimate goals of the individual practitioner.

i. Developing the Body: The body is the vehicle through which any art is expressed. The condition of that body will therefore have a tremendous impact on the art it produces. Strong practitioner should focus on exercises that increase grace and agility. Nimble students should seek to increase raw power. But all should engage in the regular process of improving and maintaining physical fitness in one fashion or another.

ii. Disciplining the Emotions: It is not easy to suppress the natural tendency to be frightened by uncertainty or danger; angered by provocation; and saddened by loss. But these negative stimuli will continue to present themselves as we move through life. One way to temper our reaction is to understand and even re-frame these experiences.

For example, when confronted by uncertainty or danger, keep the following mantra in mind:

Where am I?	Here.
When is it?	Now.
Will this pass?	It will.
Will I still be here then?	Yes.

WEI KUEN DO PRINCIPLE: YOU ARE HERE. IT IS NOW.

When confronted by provocation, know that it likely stems from the opponent's own feelings of inadequacy and that it is an invitation—and generally just an invitation— to engage at a time, and in a manner, of the opponent's choosing, and not your own.

When confronted by loss, remember that we are only sad to see something end because it was so enjoyable while it was happening, and that the memories of such things are eternal.

WEI KUEN DO PRINCIPLE: DO NOT GRIEVE BECAUSE IT IS OVER; REJOICE BECAUSE IT HAPPENED.

iii. Disengaging the Mind: Disengaging conscious thought is the key to achieving mastery in the art of Wei Kuen Do. This goal can be approached from (at least) two directions: First, you must practice your art—whatever it may be—to the point that the action itself rises up like the tide to absorb your consciousness. It is a little like reading a book or watching a film so intently that you stop "reading" or "watching" and begin simply "experiencing" the story.

Next, you must quiet your mind to the point that you submerge your conscious mind in the art. A good way to start to develop this ability is by trying to "see" with your mind and not your eyes as you fall asleep each night. Remember: The sword already knows how to cut; the bow to shoot. It is your job simply to get out of the way...

2. The Duality of Internal and External—Chi Fung:

In 1997, Master Fong was visited by representatives of Shinji Shumeikai, a Japanese organization that teaches a healing technique called "Johrei," in which practitioner use ki (energy) to heal patients. Master Fong subsequently became a Johrei practitioner himself, and, in the process, began to understand the connection between energy, healing and the martial arts. Upon this experiencing this realization, Master Fong began re-evaluating every aspect of his martial studies and ultimately developed a new training program that supplemented conventional training methods with energy exercises. By incorporating aspects of Chi Kung and Tai Chi with modern weight training techniques, Master Fong created a revolutionary system of exercise that develops functional strength, stamina and natural self-defense patterns of movement. This system, which he calls, "Chi Fung" (energy breath/wind), uses light weight dumbbells in combination with internal energy training and deep breathing, and places great emphasis on breathing in harmony with movements. The effects of this holistic approach to training have had tremendous effects on his students, from young fighters to seniors seeking renewed vitality later in life.

1. Oneness—Finding "the Zen Zone":

The ultimate goal in Wei Kuen Do is to reach the Zen state of "effortless efficiency;" fighting without fighting, and shifting from formlessness to form and then back to formlessness. In this state, the practitioner expresses his physical and technical skills, as Bruce Lee put it, "like a voice and an echo;" stimulus and response are the same. This is vital because in a real confrontation, there is no time to deliberate in deciding which technique to use. The reaction must be spontaneous. At this level, the practitioner performs the techniques instinctively, with the same ease and familiarity as such mundane tasks as driving a car or eating a meal. As Morihei Ueshiba once said in explaining his response to an attack: "I just move my mind." This kind of expertise is based not on the quantity of techniques but on the ability to express a given technique without deliberation and hesitation.

WEI KUEN DO PRINCIPLE: THOUGHT AND EXECUTION BECOME ONE.

Related to this is the idea that the student no longer "does" the technique; rather he "becomes" the technique. It is in many ways like the process through which a method actor "becomes" a character rather than simply "playing" that character. So complete is the performer's connection with his art that the boundary between the self and the performance begin to dissolve…

WEI KUEN DO PRINCIPLE: PRACTITIONER AND ART BECOME ONE.

> *It is my belief that all techniques are inadequate without the mental, emotional and spiritual dimensions. The internal structure of a self-defense system is what makes even the most implausible techniques work, while the flashy and good-looking moves fall flat without emotional content. In my own martial arts journey, I have heard scores of war stories about the trained martial artist being on the losing end of a fight with a bar room brawler. Inevitable, the same question is asked; "Why?" My answer is always the same. The brawler may have crude moves, but if he is operating from "the Zen Zone," even his awkwardness has emotional content. He is able to express his "haymaker" even though he might telegraph it from a mile away, and he can therefore make it work. The trained martial artist is accustomed to working with other trained partners, but the street fighter operates on instinct. —GMLF*

After developing the ability to operate in the Zen Zone, the practitioner can harmonize and blend with his opponent's energy, thus neutralizing the attack and following up with his own counterattacks. Every human interaction—even fighting—is an exchange of stimuli. In this way, a fight is an exchange, a communication of sorts. The key to being able to prevail is "listening" to your opponent without fear or anger and being able to adapt your responses spontaneously and appropriately.

WEI KUEN DO PRINCIPLE: ATTACKER AND DEFENDER BECOME ONE.

滙拳道

XX. FRIENDS, FAMILY, FOLLOWERS

As noted at the outset, this work is the product of the collaborative efforts of many of Grandmaster Leo Fong's friends, family, and followers. Here, then, are their own words, in their own voices:

♦ ROLLINS ALLEYNE ♦

I first met Leo in the 1970s—not in person, but I had copy of a book he had co-authored on body-building and the martial arts. At that time I was a young man seeking information on martial arts and body building, and wanted to have "the Bruce Lee" look and speed. I finally met Leo in person on my way to Las Vegas to participate in Professor Martin Buell's Kempo Karate seminar. It was around August of 2002 and I had a layover in L.A. to visit one of my former students, Norman Mayers, who was then studying with Leo in his systems: Wei Kuen Do and Chi Fung.

I was introduced to Leo by Norman at one his Chi Fung classes at the Japanese center. I remember when Norman and I showed up for the class, one of the participants asked me if I was here to teach, and was taken aback when I said that I was here to practice (maybe because of my age relative to the retired participants). The classes were not that easy, but I had a fantastic time. Immediately after the Chi Fung class, one of Leo's students went through one of the WKD Angles of Attack with us using a pair of boxing paddles. It was **amazing**, and from that point I wanted to learn to strike like that, because my first encounter with the martial arts was boxing (and I did not like getting punched in the face!). At that point I was kind of fed up with the martial arts I had been practicing for the last twenty-three years; rigid, back breaking and political.

That was the turning point for me and I decided to seek out Leo Fong's immense wisdom, not just in martial arts but in his entire life-warrior curriculum. His book on how to love unloved people made a big impact on me. In fact, one of the most remarkable things about this man of God is that he is always sharing something with you—whether it is a book, an article, a DVD, or a health thought—while others are always trying to sell you something…

On my return to Barbados after a two week visit to the USA, I decided that I was going to invite Leo to Barbados. I did know how I was going to accomplish the funding, but I knew I was going to bring this legendary master to the island. One thing Leo asked me was whether there were any typhoons (I guess he probably experienced those during his time in the Philippines). I told him that our hurricane season was very short, and the hurricanes were a small ones. In other words, I lied! I just wanted to get him to Barbados so I could learn those Angles of Attack at any price!

He finally agreed and came in November, right at the end of the hurricane season. At one point there was some tremendous flooding close to his hotel and I was scared because I only have a little car. "Oh Lord," I thought, "I am going to get Leo and his wife caught in a street flood!" But thankfully it all worked out in the end…

♦ Malcolm Boutwell ♦

Meeting the living legend, Leo Fong, is like being caught in a time warp from the past. When meeting with Leo Fong for the first time you feel like you are encountering a priest on the grounds of the Shaolin Temple, hundreds of years ago. You feel like you have been transported back in time, suddenly standing on the grounds of a monastery in the early morning, on a majestic mountain top, surrounded by pagodas. And there is

Professor Fong going through his paces in the courtyard of the temple, as the morning sun comes up.

But you would not see Professor Fong doing flowery or flashy forms in this early morning workout. You would see him merging with the beautiful view on the mountain top, as he shoots lightning fast jabs, hooks, crosses, backfists, traps, sweeps and front kicks. What you see is mind, body, and spirit with East meeting West. For in Professor Fong's journey, that began long ago, East and West have been merged together in his path.

At times Professor Fong might seem like a Shaolin Priest, but at other times he might come across as a renegade monk. When you talk to Leo Fong, you immediately realize that you are talking to a wise man, who walks a sacred path in life. But although Leo Fong might transport you to a time and place hundreds or even thousands of years into the past, he talks with an Arkansas accent; a rather noticeable dichotomy. His voice sounds a little like John Wayne, but coming out of a man who reminds you of a Shaolin Priest. But at the same time, his Eastern art is also Westernized, and you immediately recognize that it has its roots in Western Boxing.

♦ Klein Buen ♦

I first met Leo Fong in 1996, at St. Paul's United Methodist Church in Tarzana when he was a guest speaker there. My martial arts journey began when I joined his Modern Escrima classes at the fellowship hall. After about a year I was introduced to Wei Kuen Do as well.

To me, Wei Kuen Do isn't just a martial art; it is a way of living. One of the many lessons I've learned from Leo was never to be in the direct line of a strike. The same can be said about problems in life. Leo teaches that instead of confronting those issues straight on, which could be overwhelming, you should consider different "Angles of Attack." One of my favorite quotes that Leo often refers to is by Abraham Lincoln. If you've been fortunate enough to be around Leo for a long time, you've probably heard this quote quite a bit. *"Give me six hours to chop down a tree and I will spend the first four hours sharpening the axe."* This quote pretty much sums up Wei Kuen Do's four stages of growth and progress. You first sharpen the axe by developing and refining the tools, then finally chop down the tree by dissolving and expressing the tools.

Grandmaster Leo Fong is one of the most generous and humble men I know. Leo has been a close friend, teacher and mentor, as well as a father figure. He is the epitome of a great martial arts master. He often says that Jesus Christ is the greatest martial artist because he was able to fulfill his destiny through compassion, discipline and honor. Everyone close to Leo certainly knows that he has all three traits.

Leo is one of the most influential people in my life. I'm so thankful for his willingness to share his knowledge and journey in martial arts and in life. I've been blessed by his presence and I will forever be grateful.

♦ **LINDA BUSTAMANTE** ♦

Mr. Leo Fong has worn many hats—martial artist, minister, filmmaker, author, father, and husband to name a few—but the one role that is dear to my heart has been the amazingly true friend he has been to me throughout the years. Mr. Fong has been my mentor in many different facets of my life. Martial arts-wise, he has shown me that the ultimate goal in any art is finding your path and making it your own. Bruce Lee's philosophy, "I fear not the man who has practiced 10,000 kicks once, but I fear the man who has practiced one kick 10,000 times," is a concept Mr. Fong instills by being proficient in one technique before moving on to another one; this concept can transcend into different aspects of life by perfecting one task/activity/goal first before moving onto the next venture in life.

As for film, he has shown me that there are no limitations to making a film; he makes what he can with the resources he has and if you have a passion for acting or filmmaking, he guides you to following their passions and dreams.

Writing has been another part of Mr. Fong's life in which he has had the ability to be completely expressive. The origins of his writing came from the assistance of Bruce Lee. Bruce recommended to the founder of *Black Belt Magazine*, Mitoshi Uyehara, that he should have Leo Fong on the cover because he thought it was fascinating that Mr. Fong was a preacher and at the same time a martial artist. Mr. Fong's first national magazine cover story with Black Belt Magazine came out on the November 1970 issue, and, after that beginning, he has produced a plethora of written works over the last forty years. He has shown me that writing is not solely based on grammatical form, but rather on diction and substance as well. As an individual who was very self-conscious of writing, with Mr. Fong's guidance, working on collaborative articles, and interviewing him on numerous occasions, I have found writing to be the best way to chronicle all of life's most precious and timeless moments; Mr. Fong helped me find my own voice through writing.

As a human being, the two virtues I admire most about Mr. Fong, amongst many others, are his humility and selflessness. In the time I have had the pleasure of knowing the Fong family, they are the most humble and giving individuals who have shown nothing but kindness, compassion, and love to my family. The Fong family are definitely an extension of the Bustamante family and I am thankful for the blessing of having their friendships. Whether it has been reading Mr. Fong's yearly inspirational books, which he has sent me every year, or his martial arts books, I have come to find that the physical aspect is important but the spiritual aspect of the journey is his priority. His inspirational books have shown the multifaceted individual he is through all his life experiences and has given me the opportunity to learn more about the man I know as my dear friend.

Through Fongline, World Black Belt Articles and FMA Informative articles, each one of his written pieces has been informative and given the reader insight to all the different components that make up Leo Fong's life. Exploring Fongline throughout the years has given me in-depth knowledge about his arts and reading and writing articles on Mr. Fong for World Black Belt and FMA Informative has provided a wealth of knowledge, not only for my writing, but also for getting to know a man who has overcome many obstacles and achieved much in his life personally and professionally.

Mr. Fong has a fire that burns brightly for life; he cherishes every day and treats each day as a new day. One of the mottos that he lives by that holds great meaning for me is: *"What the mind can conceive and believe, it can achieve."* Through Mr. Fong's teaching I felt a closeness to that saying and made it my own, and came up with my own motto, "If you believe in your goals and dreams, then there are no such things as impossibilities, but rather infinite possibilities." This is just one example of the influence Mr. Fong has had on my life. He will continue to be a trailblazer for all to emulate his tenacity, dedication, commitment, and innovation for future generations to come. With much love and respect...

♦ CESAR CHAPARRO ♦

My Leo Fong story begins around 1976 when I was about five years old. The world was in the height of the Kung Fu craze, and I spent almost every weekend begging my father to take the family to a downtown L.A. movie house to watch the latest Kung Fu flick. I was fortunate enough to be surrounded by strong males who were very positive influences on me. We lived in Los Angeles and were exposed to many cultures there. Every continent is strongly represented in Southern California and, along with all the Mexican immigrants and African Americans from the Southern U.S., there is a multitude of people here from all over Asia.

滙拳道

My father trained for a short period at the Tenri Judo Dojo and my Uncle Gustavo earned his black belt under James Ibrau, one of Ed Parker's first black belts. Visiting my uncle was always a treat for me because he loved the fact that I loved martial arts. He knew about the latest chopsocky film and he would entertain me with his latest Kung Fu form. He had a homemade punching bags with legs and arms, homemade weights, and the largest collection of martial arts books I had ever seen. His home was like the Mexican Shaolin Temple, but right in the middle of Los Angeles! Going to his house was like walking into Toys-R-Us for me. I would 'play' Kung Fu all day long.

One day he allowed me to pick a book from his collection. I looked through them all and zeroed in on one with a maroon cover. Some poor guy was being knocked off his feet by a Chinese gentleman with a crew cut. That book was Choy Li Fut Kung Fu by Sifu Leo Fong. It was the very first martial arts book I ever owned and today it is **the** treasure in my own martial arts library. I started working on my horse stance from then on. I never realized standing still would be so hard! I even wore the crew cut, just like Leo Fong!

In my five year old head, I always thought that Leo Fong lived on the other side of the world, somewhere in the Canton Province in China. As I grew older, I was flipping through a martial arts magazine one day and read a short story about Leo Fong and assumed that he lived somewhere in Northern California. If I had been paying closer attention I would have realized that he only lived on the other side of the City, right in the San Fernando Valley.

To my surprise, in 2010 I was given the opportunity to train with Leo Fong—one of the pioneers of martial arts. My first day of training under Sifu Fong and his students was like walking into the Shaolin Temple, except this time in the San Fernando Valley. I was practicing Kung Fu, but this time I was learning all the combative applications of the movements. It was a long way from horse stance training I did when I was five—I was now learning Wei Kuen Do, an art that integrated Chinese, Filipino and American ideas into something unique in and of itself.

In writing this submission, I thought about some of the most valuable lessons Sifu Fong has shared with me. He likes to use acronyms or short phrases to help remember the main idea of the lesson. A few that come to mind are: "RSVP" (Relaxation, Slow-motion, Visualization and Pausing); "stay alert and stay alive;" "Be in the moment, it is a gift; that's why it's called 'the present'".

One particular lesson that stands out for me came about when we were having lunch during a hard morning training session at the First International Wei Kuen Do Festival of Martial Arts in 2012. It had been a particularly hard time in my life and I asked Sifu Fong, "How do you deal with all the stress and the butterflies in your stomach when you can see tough times ahead?" I guess he saw that I was expecting some type of metaphysical answer that had to do with ancient chi gung techniques. As he ate his sandwich, he looked at me and said *"Well Cesar, you suffer, but you suffer* ***through*** *it. We all have our crosses to bear. Embrace your cross and suffer through it, but always know that you are not alone."* That was a very valuable lesson indeed… God bless Sifu Leo Fong and all my martial arts brothers and sisters.

♦ Suzanne John Dillman ♦

Over the years being the wife of George Dillman I have traveled the world meeting many martial arts greats. Leo Fong stands out as so knowledgeable; every time I am around his teachings, I am in awe. He is definitely the pinnacle among teachers!

汇拳道

♦ Steven Dowd ♦

Let us start at the beginning: I was in the U.S. Navy stationed in the Philippines and was looking to get a book published. I had written to several publishing companies, and the only answer I got back was from Koinonia Productions, owned by Leo Fong. Mrs. Fong wrote to me telling me that Leo Fong was in Manila and would see me. So I drove to Manila, to the hotel where Leo was staying (he was starring in and producing *Ninja Assassin*). After meeting Leo we went up to his room to talk and I showed him the book I had been working on. Leo took a brief look, threw it on the table and said, *"What else do you know?"* I told him I knew Kuntaw from the Lanada family and he told me to put something together about that. So it was Leo who eventually published my first book "Kuntaw—The Filipino art of Hand and Foot Fighting, Volume One".

Since that time Leo and I kept in touch while I was moving around Southeast Asia in the Navy. Upon retiring and moving to San Diego, Leo and I would talk often on the phone. Leo was the first person to ask me to do a seminar (in New York); we flew there together and had a great four days of teaching, discussing and learning about each other on a more personal level.

A few years later Leo asked me to come to Los Angeles and be in a movie called, *Transformed*. I spent approximately four or five days together with him, discussing things in general in between shots. The funny thing about the movie *Transformed* is that my part was with Fred "The Hammer" Williamson who was teaching Leo's character Arnis de Mano. When the movie finally came out, my picture was on the back cover with Fred Williamson and I was listed in the credits a couple times, but when you watch the movie, if you blink, you will miss me, and all you will see of me is my right hand and forearm! It seems the film's editor did not care for my look in the film so I ended on the cutting room floor except for one brief glimpse of my right hand and forearm. The joke is that my right hand and forearm are now famous!

Through the years Leo and I have done a few seminars and gotten together in person and discussed various things, including his relationship with Bruce Lee as well as some other actors, writers and friends that he has known. I have never been a student of Leo's; he has had respect for what I teach and does not push his art on me, as I do not push my art on him. We have, I believe, a mutual respect towards each other's capabilities. Leo Fong is a person who I hold in high esteem and a true friend who, through the years, has helped me in many ways. I have always been, and will always be, here for him...

♦ Chad Dulin ♦

I first met Leo Fong at an open house at George Dillman's old Reading dojo—this would have been the mid-90s I guess. Subsequent to that I had the opportunity to train with him several times at Chas Terry's old Drexel Hill school, the University of Pennsylvania Club, and at the Deer Lake camp. I suppose it is instructive to look at Sifu Fong both as a person, and as a martial artist; the latter involving both his attributes and the system he has developed.

Having lived many years in the deep south I find Sifu Fong's accent and demeanor to be entirely charming. Despite his many, many accomplishments he remains, at his core, a southern gentleman and minister. I suspect that these are his most treasured accomplishments. He is soft spoken, self-effacing, and very polite, yet when he speaks his eyes glow with passion.

He is a grand story-teller, whether through the martial arts films he makes, or sitting quietly and listening to him speak of his time training with Bruce Lee, or Angel Cabeles or Remy Presas. A favorite story I have heard a time or two involves a conversation with Bruce Lee: Bruce had asked Leo why he was always studying this or that art, why he kept adding on. Leo replied that he was *"looking for the ultimate!"* Bruce answered "Man—you already have it in you!" And it is with this conversation that I want to turn to Leo Fong's art and what I have taken from it.

The relationship between the Filipino fighting arts and western boxing is a favorite topic for martial arts debate, as is the role of the western arts of boxing and fencing in arts generated by Bruce Lee's studies. Among other things Leo was an accomplished boxer when he met Bruce, to the point that Bruce told him **not** to use his trademark southpaw lead. The idea was, "why change what works?"

When I trained with Leo from the mid-90s to the early 2000s several things stuck with me. He has a relaxed, effortless movement, but he can weight dynamically on impact before floating away once again. On a drop step he literally causes walls to shake! The most important take-away for me, though, was his blending of Filipino style footwork with simple boxing techniques and combinations. Evolving from a simple left lead to incorporate shifting and switching leads, trapping, and various, um, unsanctioned blows, his Wei Kuen Do provides a dynamic platform for integrating Southeast Asian, Chinese, and Western arts.

The last major takeaway I want to touch on is Sifu Fong's use of what I call blind angles. In training he works numerous combinations involving an uppercut to the body followed by any variety of second and third shots. Working with him directly, and then developing these technique sets with my students really opened my eyes to sub-plots in the material left by the late Remy Presas. And that, maybe, is the connection that resonates with me. Leo trained with Remy in the Philippines; later he taught with him on some occasions. I am grateful that Sifu Fong provided me the insights he did, and that I have been able, on some level, to use his teachings and his art to blend with and deepen my own martial expression.

WEI KUEN DO

♦ Ross Dworkin ♦

Having not yet earned a black belt in Ryukyu Kempo and being new to Wei Kuen Do, it was probably a little premature for me to embark on a journey to meet the grandmaster, Leo T. Fong, but I guess one of the benefits of being a bit older is you do what you want. I was visiting the west coast for business, and not knowing the next time I'd be near Los Angeles, there was no way I was going to pass up the opportunity to meet one of the great Grandmasters.

I knew that Leo was the creator of Wei Kuen Do, an actor in several martial arts movies, and a boxer at one point. I had no idea what to expect upon meeting or working out at his dojo. I knew from growing up that some of the kids who were good at boxing were also belligerent or quick tempered. I also held the opinion that Wei Kuen Do was one of the more realistic forms of self-defense because it built upon the most basic and brutal instinct: punching someone in the head. Accordingly, I held preconceived notions of Leo's disposition, assuming that reports of his "kind and gentle nature" were based partially on his age and the admiration of his students.

In preparation for my trip, I made sure I knew the first seven "Angles of Attack;" key principles of his fighting style. I wanted to make sure that if I got a chance to work out at Leo's dojo, I could keep up with the other students. In fact—and I'm embarrassed to admit this—I had decided if that if there was sparring, I was going to fully participate. I had heard that west coast rappers were tougher than those on the East coast and I hoped the same wasn't true for martial artists! After all, I didn't want to embarrass my dojo, MKA Karate, or our master, Dr. Charles Terry.

滙拳道

After checking into my hotel room, I contacted one of Leo's colleagues, Adam James. While there were ample opportunities to meet and work out with Leo, I decided to wait until I had concluded my business. Adam instructed me to meet with Leo at a Methodist church in Sherman Oaks, California on Saturday to participate in a session of "Chi Fung." I had no idea what Chi Fung was, but I knew that there were some martial art disciplines based in tai chi and figured this was one. What I couldn't figure out was the choice of location, and just assumed it was Grandmaster Fong reaching out to the community.

I arrived at the church early to see Leo pulling a box of very light dumbbells from his trunk. I immediately parked and ran over to him at the back of his car to introduce myself. Smiling, Leo thanked me for coming to see him and then, at my insistence, I grabbed the box of light dumbbells and we proceeded towards the church. During our walk into the church, I asked Leo about Chi Fung. He explained it as a series of exercises comprised of slow movements and concentrated breathing techniques designed to promote well-being. He explained that it reduces stress, lowers blood pressure and is part of a healthy living regimen.

When we got to the church, we entered a classroom with three or four rows of chairs, arranged in a semi-circle. Already, half a dozen students were there. Over the next ten minutes, an additional ten to fifteen people arrived. Of these students, more than half were women and, with the exception of me and another woman, they were all at least seventy-five years old. Most of them were planning to use water bottles in lieu of dumbbells.

I don't remember all the exercises we did, but most of them were performed while seated and involved relaxed movements with deep and controlled breathing, all choreographed at the direction of Leo. One of our first exercises consisted of sitting comfortably while very slowly curling the arms while holding weights (either dumbbells or water bottles), breathing deeply with the diaphragm, and when the weights reached the shoulders, pausing for a few seconds, then turning the palms down (in a circular motion), and lowered the weights almost as slowly while exhaling. We did this ten times, and it was extremely relaxing.

The rest of the exercise regimen continued in a similar fashion. When exercising our legs, we stood up from our chairs slowly while breathing deeply, pausing once erect, and then slowly sitting back down, pausing and repeating several times. We did these types of exercises for almost an hour, lifting the weights over our head, similar to a shoulder press; we leaned forward while extending the arm behind the back to strengthen the triceps. We covered all of the major moving body parts, all while in a relaxed state, moving slowly and breathing deeply. During these exercises, many of the seniors engaged in light and pleasant conversation, usually about grandchildren. The entire experience was pleasant; in fact the atmosphere alone would have reduced stress and lowered everyone's blood pressure. In addition to lower blood pressure, everyone agreed that Chi Fung helped them sleep better as well.

It is easy to see why Leo is in demand, running ten classes a week. In fact it's hard to understand why Chi Fung isn't ubiquitous. At the conclusion of the class, I got to speak with some of the participants and watch them interact with Leo. At that point, it was far easier to see Leo as a minister than an actor or grandmaster. It was apparent that he was delighted to help these people feel better and, despite the adulation he received from them, there was no condescension or patronization in the way he spoke to them. He was simply a kind, sincere man, spreading joy.

Afterwards, I was able to convince Leo and his wife, Minnie, to join me for lunch. During our time together, Leo recounted stories of his upbringing in Arkansas and some of the challenges he faced as a boy from China being bullied, which was what motivated him to start boxing. However, most fascinating were his recollections from his days making karate movies in the seventies and eighties. Leo worked with some well-known stars like Richard Roundtree, Cameron Mitchel (who introduced him to Minnie), Fred Williamson and others. Leo traveled the world making these movies and he didn't just star in them; in many cases he produced, directed and wrote them.

Since my time with Leo I have maintained contact with him via email and his Facebook page. I've come to realize that you cannot look at Leo as two figures: A kind, gentle minister *or* a marital artist/actor. Leo is simply a God-fearing man with great integrity who does everything as well as he can. Because his character never allows him to quit, he always improves and therefore has conquered a great many challenges. The real Leo Fong is best described as a member of the human race whose kind, gentle ways are cherished and appreciated; a man who is an inspiration to all who know him.

♦ Juliana Ehnot ♦

It has been an honor and a pleasure to train with one of the world's most influential Grandmasters. Leo Fong's philosophy on life and the martial arts is an inspiration to many. His willingness to share his knowledge will assure that Wei Kuen Do continues to be an important part of the martial arts for generations to come. I am so proud and honored to help continue and pass along this tradition. Thank you so much Grandmaster Fong.

♦ Will Higginbotham ♦

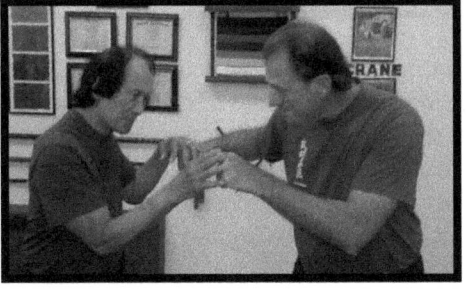

My first involvement with Grandmaster Leo Fong was in the Fall of 1996 when I met him in Reading, Pennsylvania at the one of Professor Dillman's events. At that time he was in his late sixties and I was only in my mid-forties. I was blown away with how he moved and how young he appeared. Since then I have had the pleasure of training under him many times at the Muhammad Ali Camp and one time in LA about ten years ago.

I don't have a story of my own, but instead one that Leo told me last Fall. We are all interested in stories about Bruce Lee. I was asking about training with him and how he may have influenced Bruce. Leo said he was training with Bruce one day and was asking him what some of the Wing Chun moves meant. He said that when Bruce's answer didn't satisfy him, he told Bruce that they needed to spar. When he sparred Bruce, he said that Bruce couldn't hit him. That sparring session is what drove Bruce to look into western boxing. When Leo next saw Bruce, he said that Bruce met him at the door carrying a box of 8mm movies of Muhammad Ali fights. It is obvious that Leo had a very practical influence on the formation of Bruce Lee's art.

♦ JESSICA HOBART ♦

When you train in anything, you become very fond of the people with whom you train, whether it be a class in Chinese Kung Fu or cooking. I do, however, believe that your comrades in martial arts are a little different. They are more than your friends; they are your family, with your peers being your siblings, your direct teachers being your parents, and your masters being your grandparents or great grandparents. You never want to let those people down. One of the masters at my dojo is Leo Fong. Though I do not see him very often, and we are not related by blood, we are family. I want him to see me excel, just as most students do. His being like a grandfather inspires me and my peers to do better; to try to be good people. Martial arts isn't about your next belt; it's about being better you. Leo Fong and Wei Kuen Do motivate me do be a better student, and a better person.

唔該 Sifu Fong, for all of your valuable lessons and teachings.

汇拳道

◆ JEFF JEDS ◆

I met Leo Fong in July 2011. Our first meeting was at a Starbucks in Sherman Oaks. Marc Lawrence, a fellow martial artist, introduced us. I must admit I was star-struck the first time I met Leo Fong. I never knew that such a legend lived around my city block. I sat next to him and he began talking about his experience living in the Philippines. He then carried on with the stories about his friendship with Bruce Lee, Linda Lee, James Lee and his life coming to the United States having to deal with racism.

He also spoke about his movie career as an actor and a film producer. I was fascinated with his stories. Then, before we parted ways, I told to him that he should make a film about his life. He replied that he has ideas and he plans to do so. We then exchanged phone numbers and agreed to meet the following week. Thereafter, we continued to have our weekly meetings and discussions on martial arts and filmmaking. After a few weeks, Leo began to coach me on fight choreography and basic acting. He told me that the best way to practice is hands on. He decided to start filming different scenes, including fight scenes. It was an exciting and fun experience.

After several weeks of continuous discussion and comparison of our martial arts styles, I got curious about his system, "Wei Kuen Do: the Way of the Integrated Fist." I was amazed to discover that it shared the same principles as my own system—Jedokan: the Way to Versatility and Self-Actualization. They have very similar footwork and body mechanics, and our training methods both focus on being elusive, adaptable, and versatile. We agree on the importance of freestyle sparring and staying away from too much compliant forms of training. After learning that we shared so much in common, I asked him if he would take me as a student. Leo Fong is so humble and considerate of other's status that he told me to just consider him as a training partner rather than a Sifu because I am also a martial arts founder. I was so inspired and humbled by his comment that I wanted to be considered his student all the more! We finally agreed that I would be both his student and training partner.

Leo Fong is a man of wisdom, skill and compassion. He has faced different types of trials in life and experienced a fair amount of sorrow and joy. However, what impresses me the most about Leo is his sincere trust in what the Creator can do for men. When he tells me stories about his past that either end in happiness or despair, he always concludes that the Creator allowed things to happen for a reason. He often uses Biblical stories when giving advice. He frequently refers to my favorite Bible character, King David, when we are discussing courage versus fear. He likens King David to a man of honor and courage but above all, someone who trusts in the Almighty Creator. Then he likens Goliath to life's troubles and problems. Most of his analogies are inspirational.

There were many occasions when I was going through tough times and Leo would motivate me to carry on. He hates seeing others down. He is always ready to lend a helping hand. Leo Fong is an optimist; he has a good heart and a way with words that can brighten your worst days.

Leo Fong has many students and followers all around the world. It is fair to say that, although we share the same basic training in Wei Kuen Do, we each have different interpretations and ways of applying the art. Wei Kuen Do to me is the combination of Bruce Lee's and Leo Fong's principles. Leo told me the story about a conversation he had with Bruce. Bruce asked Leo why he practices in different styles. Leo told Bruce he was seeking for the ultimate. Then, Bruce pointed at Leo's chest and told him the ultimate is in there. Bruce advised him to master and expand what he already knew. As a result, Leo established WKD based on his training and experiences both in the streets and in the ring. Leo told me to follow Bruce's advice but to keep in mind not to accumulate, not to imitate, but instead to **integrate** and this is the basic belief of Wei Kuen Do. I believe that Jeet Kune Do: the Way of the Intercepting Fist and Wei Kuen Do: the Way of the Integrated Fist play major roles in the advancement of Jedokan: the Way of the Versatile Warrior.

My training with Wei Kuen Do has helped me improve my boxing skills. It has also given me ideas to develop new training drills, both defensive and offensive. The footwork and body mechanics of WKD teach an individual to be evasive with quick counter-attacks. The system is composed of ten Angles of Attack with boxing strikes and footwork as the basic foundation.

After learning the Ten Angles of Attack, the student will then move into Trap Boxing, Circles of Destruction and other, advanced training drills.

Leo Fong also developed a drill using foam padded sticks as target mitts. This type of drill helps students actualize what Leo Fong refers to as "DRATT," which stands for: D-Distance, R-Relax Focus, A-Angles, T-timing, and T-Target. We also practice a lot of semi-prearrange, non-contact and contact sparring in WKD, which helps enhance our reflexes. In my own system, I refer to this as RDT, which stands for R-Reflex, D-Development, and T-Training. These drills are non-compliant and are designed to enhance a person's reflexes to be reactive with accuracy and timing.

The way Leo Fong designed WKD is with simplicity and efficiency. The art is not complicated to learn and anyone who had previous experience in other systems can easily adapt to the drills. WKD is a martial arts style that enhances students abilities, regardless of what discipline they are practicing. Wei Kuen Do is an effective and a practical style of martial arts.

The future of WKD is looking bright. Leo and I decided to merge together and utilize the Jedokan-WKD center as our Headquarters. The union of Jedokan and Wei Kuen Do helps both systems to innovate. We continuously develop new training drills which involve both empty hand and weapons. We teach classes on a weekly basis and we also conduct seminars together. Leo and I plan to film new instructional videos and write new books. We are looking forward to future seminars throughout the United States and other countries. It is our objective to expand our group and certify qualified instructors around the world. Our team will persistently teach what is factual and effective with sincerity and love for the art and our fellow martial artists.

♦ Tania Koolen ♦

I first met Dale Speedy, Sixth Dan black belt in Judo, several years ago. He is a master of his own development—"Flinchlock Release Therapy"—here in New Zealand. I am training to become a Flinchlock Release practitioner. In one of the classes Dale gave me some exercises that were called, "Leo Fong exercises." Dale speaks of Leo with great respect and honor. I use these exercises, along with Flinchlock Release Therapy, every day to heal myself. Through these exercises I started to find balance and ease with myself.

Dale said he met Leo at a conference thirty years ago, and Leo told him, *"If you are sick, there are certain exercises you need to do before anything else every day."* It was the Leo Fong exercises that changed my life and helped me to get to where I am today, and I have deep respect and honor for Leo Fong, a man I have never met, but know in my heart has changed many lives, not just mine. My journey to where I am now, I think, started with Leo Fong. Dale would not be the person he is to day, nor would I, without him. Leo Fong has touched many hearts, and his respect and honor have a flow-on effect.

♦ SHANE LEAR ♦

I am always intrigued by martial artists who stand the test of time; teachers who stay active, teaching lessons to the younger generation about what they have learned in their martial journeys—they are like encyclopedias of knowledge. Leo Fong is one such teacher. I grew up reading about Leo in martial arts publications and finally had the great pleasure of meeting him in 2011.

The first thing that struck me was his tremendous ability at his impressive age. He rarely stops moving for a long period of time! His dedication to the arts he has developed—Wei Kuen Do and Chi Fung—is only rivaled by the wisdom he shares with his students about life in the arts. An extraordinary martial artist, Leo walks the walk through his practice regimen, leading the next generation by example. I am proud to call Leo Fong my teacher, my mentor, and my friend!

♦ Lee Lollio ♦

Whatever I say about Leo Fong, the words wouldn't be sufficient enough, because the man has done so much for me as my teacher, mentor, business partner, but most importantly, my very close friend who I consider family. Ironically, I grew up idolizing Leo Fong on the big screen, because I was a huge fan of martial arts action films ever since I stepped into my first dojo as a precocious eight year old (who has been hooked on martial arts ever since). I felt I knew Leo years before I met him in person. I first saw him at the age of twelve at the local movie theater in my hometown in the suburbs of Detroit, Michigan. It was the Allen Park Theater; the same theater where I saw *Enter the Dragon,* starring the late, great Bruce Lee, and many other now classic martial art films I was so enthralled with.

Leo was starring in an independent, major hit, and now cult classic film: *Killpoint.* I also saw another one of his movies, *Low Blow,* now also a cult classic, at that same movie theater. I would never have thought in my wildest dreams that years later I would meet the great Leo Fong in person, and that he would exceed all my expectations and become my mentor in so many avenues in life.

Since becoming a student, and later a close friend, of Grandmaster Fong I have experienced so much with him and I am grateful for every minute of it, and definitely much wiser for it. I have been fortunate to work on films with him and also to travel and have the honor of teaching beside him at seminars. But what I cherish the most is our one-on-one time when we are training together or when he's sharing his life experiences with me. Being a former golden gloves boxer like Leo I love it when he shares his memories of the ring in the golden age of boxing. The man has lived several incredible, lives and has been successful and productive in every one of them, but more importantly he has touched so many people's lives, like mine and many others, for the better.

Leo Fong and I also share a very strong spiritual bond as devout Christians and witnesses for Christ, he as an ordained minister and me as an ordained deacon. We have very similar beliefs and, for the most part, do not—as the proverbial saying goes—wear our Christianity on our sleeves, but rather show our faith through our works and our respect for every person's journey in life, Christian or not.

I would like to share a story about something that Leo Fong did for me that meant so much, that I will never forget, and for which I will be in debt to him for all my days: Several years ago I had a serious health setback and was under a doctor's care. I was deemed unable to drive as a result of my ailment and had my driver's license revoked for a couple months until I was fit enough with a clean bill of health from the doctor and cleared to drive again. While in recovery and off work, in and out of doctors and specialist offices on a weekly basis, I wasn't able to go and train with Leo because I wasn't able to drive. When Leo found out about my condition, he told me not to stress over it and that through faith and prayer, everything would be back to normal in no time.

He also started driving to my home on a weekly basis to continue training me, so that I could keep up with our training, but also to visit me to offer encouragement and friendship. What made this kindness especially remarkable was the fact that my home was about an hour away from his at the time, and he was 80 plus years old. To even consider having him drive that far on a weekly basis just to see me was more than I could ever ask and I discouraged it, but he insisted and made the trip to my home for several weeks until I was able to drive again. Leo doing this extraordinary thing despite his age and busy schedule teaching classes almost every day is something I will never forget. The compassion he showed me is what a true teacher-student relationship and friendship is all about.

I am proud to be a part of the Wei Kuen Do and Chi Fung family. We choose to use the term "family" instead of "organization" because Grandmaster Fong has always emphasized a family dynamic rather than using a corporate organizational concept. Our select group may be small compared to some other martial arts organizations, but this is purposeful because our members are of the highest quality, led by a special man of faith and strong character in Grandmaster Leo Fong. I am so excited to see what is on the horizon for the future of the Wei Kuen Do family...

♦ Richard Meagher ♦

I remember my first test with Grandmaster Leo Fong. At the time, I was still very new to Wei Kuen Do. While I was practicing the physical movements of the Ten Angles of Attack every day, and was getting very comfortable with the techniques, I had not learned much about the philosophy of Wei Kuen Do. The only exposure I had to the philosophical foundation of the system was through Grandmaster Fong's books. On the day of the test, I was asked to lead two other individuals testing through the Ten Angles of Attack. We ran through all ten as a set, but in between each set of ten, Grandmaster Fong would tell us a story that pertained to an element of the philosophy of Wei Kuen Do. The test turned into a three hour private lesson for me and the others testing. It was a remarkable experience.

He shared with us training methods, the principles of D.R.A.T.T., the importance of integration, and even some of the history of the system. I will never forget the lessons he shared that day. He is an amazing individual and an inspiration to martial artists everywhere. I am immensely grateful to Grandmaster Leo Fong for his teachings and to Sensei Shane Lear for continuing to guide me through my journey in Wei Kuen Do.

WEI KUEN DO

♦ JOHN MIRRIONE ♦

Like Leo's, my martial arts training began in response to bullying. As a result, I understand that stopping such negative energy—with your hands or your words—can bring you to a higher level of consciousness. It's not about overkill, because that risks having you become the bully; it's about learning to use just enough force to stop the attack.

I first learned about Leo Fong through Adam James, who I had met at a martial arts event in Atlantic City. I first met Leo in person at the Black Belt Hall of Fame ceremony in California in 2006. When I met Leo, I already had extensive martial arts experience—I knew how to move—so my training with Leo started from that point. Right away I recognized that Leo and I shared certain beliefs, including the importance of personal integrity, the role of healing in the martial arts, and the value of learning to be still, move slowly and breathe.

Many martial arts students like things fast and think that it has to hurt to be good. While I embrace the UFC because of the truth it brings to the martial arts community, I have concerns about its violent aspects. I believe that it is important that endeavors like the UFC be integrated with spiritual conditioning in order to produce a complete awakening and understanding in the student. The martial arts are a lifetime endeavor, and they offer more than ways to knock people out. Combat effectiveness needs to be combined with such internal practices as the yoga modalities. Recently, I have started to see a shift in the martial arts community toward this ideal.

Just as Bruce Lee affected Leo Fong by telling him to seek the ultimate within, Leo once told me that in my martial arts practice it was important to "be yourself," and I think this advice had the same effect on me that it had on Leo. Leo teaches that there are four stages in the evolution of the martial artist. In the beginning, the student learns to develop his tools. He learns first to stand; then to stand and move; and then to stand, move, and strike. As the movements start to become instinctive, the student is engaged in the process of refining these tools. Once the student has developed and refined the tools, he can begin to express them. To my way of thinking, expressing the tools has two aspects: the physical and the spiritual.

On the physical side, you express the tools by being formless in your techniques. Your forms (kata) are valuable teaching tools, but they should refine you; not define you. On the spiritual side, when you begin to perfect your martial arts techniques, it starts to translate into every aspect of your life—your job, your relationships, etc... You start to be able to express yourself perfectly in every realm, and you begin act instinctively as opposed to mechanically. Finally, when the student achieves mastery, he begins to dissolve the tools. Leo Fong is truly such a master.

When this book was being written, I suggested to the editors that they should contact Bruce Lee's wife to talk about Leo Fong's legacy and I am very grateful that they did so and that Ms. Cadwell graciously responded. While he is undoubtedly a powerful warrior, Leo Fong's words are even more powerful than his left hook. The spiritual impact of "the man behind the movement" cannot be underestimated.

♦ SCOTT PERLO ♦

I think the thing to understand about Leo is that he's fundamentally a quiet guy, but when he's got something to say, you'll hear it! When you're working out with him, he doesn't fill the air with a lot of jabber. He is a man of great gentleness, but it wasn't always that way. He told me that from growing up Chinese in the South, he was full of anger, mostly because of the way he was treated. Once, when he was a teenager, three guys confronted him and started in—threatening, giving him a hard time and spoiling for a fight. Leo looked the ringleader in the eye and then hit his friend so hard he knocked the guy out. It so unnerved that the other two ran away!

I think that one of the best things about Leo, both as a teacher and a role model, is his incredible physical conditioning. I don't know if he was born with it, or it is the result of working out essentially every day of his life, but Leo, in his 70s, was significantly faster and stronger than I was, in my twenties and in my prime.

One time, Leo was demonstrating a combination for me, and he moved a faster than I had expected. By which I mean that one moment he was there, and the next he was *over there*. I had been training for quite a while by then, but I still couldn't keep up with him. His uppercut connected with my jaw, and, even though he was probably only giving about 20% or 30%, it was like being hit with a steel bar!

Leo's incredible health and wellbeing extend beyond his muscles. Doctors found a benign tumor during one of his checkups, and Leo went in to have it removed. It wasn't a small deal, and the surgery would have kept most people out of commission for at least a week, if not more. Leo was working out the next day. It wasn't much—just walking through the mall and lifting light weights, but whatever he can do—that's what Leo always does.

I think that Leo sees the martial arts as a combination of very simple and straightforward movements and a great deal of thinking and understanding. A lot of our training was talking and listening. Especially as time went on, we'd work a combo, and then Leo would talk for a while, explaining why he put it together this way, what it meant to respond to an opponent, but also how to 'be' in the world. It was always interesting, and remarkable considering how quiet he was at other times. You could tell that, as a preacher, the martial arts connected his hands to his heart. He is one of the most soulful people I know.

I think that I'll always remember Leo caught in one moment, but a moment that happened over and over again: He would be demonstrating a hook and then he would just explode, switching his feet in a blur of motion. He'd land, and his fist, lightly curled, would be hanging half a millimeter away from his partner's jaw. There would be a moment of silence and then he'd start to laugh! That's Leo; the most ferociously gentle guy I know.

♦ Brit Potter ♦

I have attended multiple Leo Fong seminars over the years. The fall of 2014 was the latest seminar that I attended. Leo was 85 years 'young' at the time. During this seminar, I had the opportunity to be his *uke* and all I could think was, "I would hate for him to really hit me!" An 85 year old with the striking ability and moves of a 40 year old is just unheard of… He really impressed me and is a role model for everyone. Remember:
It's not now long you live; it's the quality of the life that counts.

♦ Andrew Reese ♦

I always seek the perfect combination and pay special attention to the finer details when it comes to the implementation and application of martial arts techniques. That is exactly get every time I train with Leo Fong…

WEI KUEN DO

♦ DUSTY SEALE ♦

I met Leo Fong at the first three day training session held by George Dillman at the Muhammad Ali camp. I was wearing Grandmaster Dillman's famous black uniform top that he is seen wearing in all his pictures. Master Fong later said he thought I was one of Grandmaster Dillman's sons because he recognized the name "Dusty," and I had the name "Dillman" across the back of my uniform. Leo used me for demonstration throughout the entire weekend. I was amazed at how he moved and how he could detect what I was going to do before I did it. By the end of the training I was really trying to hit him, just like he told me to. Each time I threw a punch, he was behind me, slapping me in the back of the head and kicking my leg! His speed was and still is truly amazing...

Later that night, after the training was over and everyone was partying and socializing, I saw Leo sitting in a chair out by the camp fire just watching the flames. I approached and asked if I could sit and talk with him. He smiled from ear to ear and invited me to sit. Man, we talked about anything and everything! Then he asked if I wanted to go into the gym and workout! So both Friday and Saturday night, while everyone else was partying, I took full advantage and was trained one-on-one by Leo Fong himself! That where the picture above is from (and why I still have hair in it!).

Leo Fong genuinely cares about you as a person and your training. To this day I talk with Leo regularly and train with him as much as possible. He and I are working on a pressure point boxing DVD series as well. Leo is a retired minister and conducted the marriage ceremony for me and my beautiful wife, Erica. He is part of my family and I am honored to be part of his martial tradition.

♦ CHRISTIAN SPITZER ♦

My name is Christian Spitzer and I have been a student of Leo Fong since 2004. Since my early childhood I was a fan of the late Bruce Lee and was therefore interested in Kung Fu. Since there was no Kung Fu in Austria at that time I started with Karate and then some other eclectic martial arts styles. In January of 1991 I began training in Wing Chun and over the years participated in several JKD seminars in Europe and the USA, and had private lessons with Jesse Glover and Ted Wong, both of whom were original Bruce Lee students.

Through my search on the internet I came across the email address of Leo Fong in 2002. I immediately contacted him and he responded promptly. Over the next few years I asked him thousands of questions and he answered all of them patiently. Our correspondence was not only through email but also via phone calls and we had some great conversations regarding Bruce Lee, JKD and of course Wei Kuen Do, Leo's own martial art.

Leo sent me several of his books and video tapes and also invited me to come to California and train with him. He told me he would take care of the accommodation and food and I would only have to pay for the airfare. I just couldn't believe that someone who had never met me in person would make such an astonishing offer! In May of 2004 I was able to fly to LA and train with Grandmaster Leo Fong. Although we had never met before, it was like seeing an old friend and I was also made very welcome by Leo's wife, Minnie.

The first day of my training started with the introduction of the Ten Angles of Attack. I still remember that when I learned Angle Number One I said to myself, "I'm never going to get it, and if I already have problems with Number One, how am I going to learn the remaining nine?" I trained up to eight hours a day for nine days and during that time I learned the entire Ten Angles of Attack and also the Ten Circles of Destruction (the defensive part of the WKD system).

Leo has students perform every technique a thousand times to make sure that they can not only perform it, but that they are certain of it. Leo's four stages of training—Developing the Tools, Refining the Tools, Dissolving the Tools and Expressing the Tools—this is the key!

During my stay in Los Angeles I met several of Leo's students, with whom I also worked out, but mostly with his two top students at that time, namely Scott Perlo and Adam James. Since my stay at Leo's I founded my own WKD group in Salzburg, Austria and have been training and teaching ever since. I made another visit to Leo in 2010 to further my progress in WKD. In 2012 I was promoted to Fifth Level and the representative for WKD in Europe. I still continue to improve my skills in WKD and I hope to be able to visit Leo in the near future.

Thank you Grandmaster Leo Fong. Words cannot describe for everything you have done for me!

♦ Dr. Steve Stewart ♦

The first time I ever met Leo Fong in person was at the very first Muhammad Ali Camp in May 2000. We shared the same cabin, and on both Friday and Saturday evening, we sat up until three or four a.m. while Leo shared story after story regarding the late great Bruce Lee. I was fascinated by what was told to me about this person and his ability as a martial artist despite various challenges: For one, Bruce was extremely nearsighted. For another, one of his legs was shorter than the other. He was only 5'7" and weighed 140 lbs.

One story that stands out in my mind was the time when Bruce called Leo up and said, "We need to take a drive." The two of them drove to a location where there was a karate school on the second floor. Bruce said to Leo, "You wait here. I'll be right back." Leo asked Bruce, *"Do you want me to go with you?"* Bruce replied, "No, I'm just going to have a chat." Then next thing Leo heard was some argument... Elevated voices... And then, "Wham! Wham! Wham!"... Then silence. The next thing Leo saw was Bruce emerging from the building. Bruce came over to the car, got in, and said, "OK, we can go now." When Leo asked Bruce what had just happened, Bruce replied, "I just had a chat and enlightened someone on the philosophy of what a true martial artist is all about. Leo asked, *"So how did he take it?"* Bruce replied, "He is going to sleep on it for a bit!" That's how Bruce did it. He would say, "Enough talk. Show me on the mat." Very few could do that...

I also remember one Saturday morning at the Ali Camp when Leo asked me if I wanted to work out together. I was thrilled. We got up at 6 a.m. and went down to the gym where I was educated on what Leo Fong had created. We went through a series drills. I was impressed with his power and speed, not to mention his sense of humor! Then we grabbed some dumbbells and started doing drills with them. Now Leo was in his mid-sixties at this time and I was only in my early forties, so when he picked up two 10 pound weights, I decided to pick up two 25 pound weights, because I was a bit younger and felt that I was in pretty good shape. As we went through the series of exercises it became clear that I was beginning to feel the heaviness and pain in my arms, shoulders and legs. Leo continued at a steady pace with a grin on his face. By the time we had completed the entire series, I was using just the two dumbbell bars with no weight and Leo was still going steady with his 10 pound weights. I was humbled that day and my respect for this exceptional individual became second to none. His words to me were: *"It's quality, not quantity Steve. Learn to pace yourself. Don't be in such a hurry. Take your time. Enjoy the moment and embrace it..."*

WEI KUEN DO

♦ LANCE STRONG ♦

I've been involved in the martial arts for 57 years and in that time have come to consider Grandmaster Leo Fong to be the embodiment of an authentic martial arts master. Not only is Leo a phenomenal martial artist, and a true innovator who has contributed a huge amount to the evolution of the arts, but he is also one of those rare individuals who is also a man great integrity, humility and spirituality.

Many martial artists have an in-depth understanding of the physical techniques of their art, but it is not so common to find a master who really understands and comprehensively applies all of the mind/body/spirit elements of the arts.

I first met Grandmaster Leo Fong when we were both staying at Grandmaster George Dillman's house in 1990. We had taken a New Zealand team to compete in Grandmaster Dillman's Northeast Karate Championships. From the first moment we sat around chatting about the martial arts and life in general, I knew that here was a man who was truly authentic in all that he did, and that I had a lot to learn from his wisdom.

Since our first meeting we kept in contact and in the mid-nineties we brought Grandmaster Fong to New Zealand, where he taught a series of highly successful seminars around our Kiaido Ryu Martial Arts Schools.

In the early 2000s I was living and working in the Topanga Canyon area in the Valley in LA, and was able to reconnect with Leo. This led to training in the park with him on Sunday mornings, and studying more of his Wei Kuen Do system, which I continue to do to this day. I will be forever grateful to Leo for sharing his knowledge, art and friendship with me.

After returning to New Zealand we returned again to LA to attend a Wei Kuen Do three-day training seminar with Grandmaster Fong and his team, including Adam James, Klein Buen and Lee Lollio. We had a fantastic time filled with fellowship and training, with a great family of martial artists from all over the world, all brought together to study with a true master and a man we are all privileged to call our dear friend.

I sometimes think that many American martial artists do not realize what an amazing resource of martial knowledge and skill, and what a treasure they have access to in Grandmaster Leo Fong. If you ever get the opportunity to study with him don't hesitate; it will make you a better martial artist and, more importantly, a better human being.

♦ **Dr. Charles Terry** ♦

I must thank Grandmaster George Dillman and Peter Hobart for my connection with Grandmaster Leo Fong. As a long-time member of DKI, senior black belts used to be awarded plaques signed by Professor Remy Presas, Professor Wally Jay, Grandmaster George Dillman, and Grandmaster Leo Fong. After attending "triple seminars" with Presas-Jay-Dillman, we became curious about the fourth Grandmaster; Leo Fong. Peter Hobart sought him out and ultimately we were able to invite Grandmaster Fong in for a seminar in the 1990s. Since then, he has shared his drive and skill with us through new partner drills, handwork, footwork, and a focus on the philosophical side of the martial arts. As an accomplished film star, his "cinematic stunt fighting" seminars have also been very popular with our students. His numerous books and films are a constant inspiration. In 2006, he was inducted into the Black Belt Hall of Fame. In 2013, he received the Remy Presas Lifetime Achievement Award and was inducted into the International Modern Arnis Foundation Hall of Fame.

I learned a lesson early on from Grandmaster Fong that he perpetually reinforces through both his actions and his words, "there is no excuse not to exercise." When I first met him at the airport, he was toting only a small suit-case. I offered to help and quickly realized it was much heavier than it looked. Apparently, he liked to travel with only a few clothes and his hand weights (so he could squeeze in a workout anytime and anyplace). Since that time, I do not recall ever seeing him sit still for long without doing some form of exercise. Years later, he and his wife, Minnie were at the Dillman/Muhammad Ali training camp. During part of the seminar I found them both in the back room catching a quick workout with some hand weights. He is the reason there is a pair of hand weights under my desk in my medical office, and the reason they get used daily.

Even though we live on opposite coasts, I was honored to have him attend my wedding in 2000. Through a speech by our best man, Peter Hobart, Grandmaster Leo Fong offered his words of wisdom:

<u>Fourteen Commandments of a Strong Marriage</u>
1. Thou shall not get mad at the same time
2. Thou shall not take it personally when of you says, "I have a headache."
3. Thou shall not try to mold the other person into your own image.
4. Thou shall learn to accept the other one as he or she is, warts and all.
5. Thou shall not work on the 50/50 theory but on the 90/10 theory.
6. Thou shall look at all disagreement as only small stuff that is not worth getting upset.
7. Thou shall never go to bed angry. Making peace always precedes making love.
8. Thou shall learn to love each other without clutching.
9. Thou shall learn to join each other without invading.
10. Thou shall criticize each other without blaming.
11. Thou shall invite each other without demanding.
12. Thou shall help each other without insulting.
13. Thou shall leave each other without guilt.
14. Thou shall never make money a major issue.

As directed by Leo, and much to the surprise of the wedding guests, Pete completed the Commandments: "Add the phrase, 'in bed!' to the end of each Commandment and read a second time!"

I have been blessed to have the guidance of Grandmaster Leo Fong for several decades. His system Wei Kuen Do. includes emphasis on the spiritual side of self-defense and the psychological aspects of the practice of martial arts He inspires with his generosity and his example. We all face adversity. Yet, this is just one part of life. It is not the only part of life. Adversity requires adaptation and perseverance. In spite of illness or injury, over-scheduling or other distractions, there is always a way to get in a workout and to seek self-improvement. His stories of the early days with Bruce Lee, Wally Jay, Remy Presas, and George Dillman are invaluable. We are proud to share the methods of Wei Kuen Do with our students.

It seems appropriate that Master Fong's family should have the last word…

♦ Bong Tumaru ♦

I will always think of my father as reverend first and martial artist second. I know that is a bit of a strange thing when referring to someone that people call, "Grandmaster." I remember times when visitors would come by and be thrilled to speak with him. Afterwards, they would look at me and say something along the lines of, "learn everything you can from this man." All the while I would be thinking to myself, "of course I am. I know how to fry catfish, steam rice, and that Sunday is when we go to church…" Honestly, the reason for this is because that is how he was introduced to me, and it is what I called him "reverend" until he married my mother. After that day, my grandmother told me that it would be acceptable to call him father from that point on.

My first glimpse into my father as a martial artist was through roughhousing. I did not see this as martial arts training; it was just having fun. My cousins would all use me for wrestling practice, and my dad would try to help by showing me ways to get stronger. I remember knuckle pushups and grip strengthening exercises (although at the time, I saw this as a game). I remember learning how to claw my way out of holds (tiger claw) and how to hit things with different parts of my hand (snake head). Again, this was not training for me. It was fun and games.

Training was never formal. In hindsight, my father seemed to be preparing me for real-world situations where the courtesy shown in the dojo would not be the norm. I remember after wrestling we had to switch to boxing because my mom was afraid that the constant tumbling around would ruin the furniture.

I knew my dad used to box, but I never understood how good he was at it until I started to step into the living room with him. At this point, I had already gotten into fights at school and was able to hold my own. I was sure that I would be able to land a few shots on my dad—nope—I could never see where his hands were coming from. I never understood why he was always just out of my reach but he could tag me easily and frequently. Whenever I backed up, I always caught one to the face. It was frustrating. There was little or no explanation at this time. It was an experience. One day in desperation, I ducked down under one of his punches and swung wildly over my head. I actually caught him in the chin. He buckled and wavered a bit. It was like that moment when you do an awesome move in a video game, but have no idea how you did it.

He said, *"That was a good one Bong! Ready for the next round?"*

Everything is a blur from there, but I am fairly sure he continued to thrash me thoroughly...

It was always real world application, but with a warning. I would always talk about kicking someone's ass because they pissed me off. At this point he would say, *"Well, you could do that but is it worth the consequences?"*

One day after class, I had a heated argument with two other students. They were mocking one of my friends and I did not appreciate it. I ended up fighting one after the other. On the first day, I won my fight against the first guy—the instigator of the whole situation. On the second day, his friend came up and asked if we were still fighting. My ego jumped right on it and accepted. During this second fight, I found I was a bit more evenly matched. The guy was a wrestler. I managed to knock him down but he countered with a headlock. The fight was at a stalemate for a bit. The hold was broken up and at that point I walked right into a punch that pushed my lip into my tooth cutting me wide open. It also split the guy's hand wide open, right down to the knuckle. He rushed to the hospital, and I kind of stood there, listening to everyone cheering. I could already hear my dad's voice asking, *"Was it worth it?"*

When I got home, I showed my dad the damage. He said, *"Yup, we're gonna have to go to the hospital to get that fixed up."* He then asked how it happened, and I told him. As I was waiting for the "Was it worth it?" I heard something different from him: *"Why did you let your guard down?"* This question definitely caught me off guard. I wasn't being questioned about the reason for the fight; I was being questioned about the fight itself. After that day, we began to talk about martial arts.

My formal training began around 2005, and that is when I was introduced to Wei Kuen Do and Chi Fung under the supervision of my father and his senior student, Adam James. It was during this time that all the little lessons from before that time started to make sense to me. I began to see the reasons behind all the little movements that were programmed into me at a young age, and to see how to implement them in various in situations. I finally had my answers.

The funny thing is that after all that time wondering and finally getting my answers, I found myself putting more emphasis on dissolving the tools and developing spontaneity. Becoming what I learned was more important that regurgitating the lessons. Integrating the techniques into my gut became more of the goal than philosophizing about strategies. Is this why my training was always action-based teaching rather than philosophical?

♦ Minerva Tumaru-Fong ♦

I have been asked to write something about my husband, Leo Fong. There is so much I could say about him, but the one thing that stands out the most is his dedication to his martial art of Wei Kuen Do. Some will talk about their martial arts, but Leo not only talks the talk; he also walk the walk. From the moment he gets up in the morning until he goes to bed at night, Leo is always working on refining his art. Some may call that fanaticism, but I prefer to think of it as dedication. I am so happy and proud that at the age of 87, his passion and enthusiasm for training has not waned.

WEI KUEN DO

XXI. THE WORDS OF THE MASTER...

Prior to his death, Bruce Lee said to me, "I am closing down all my schools. I have been offered a lot of money to open a chain of Kung Fu schools, but I have turned it down." He explained to me that Jeet Kune Do was his brand and he feared that many who adopted the name would not do it justice. I understood.

When Bruce passed in 1973, I was in Hong Kong with Chaplin Chang, who worked on with him on 'Enter the Dragon.' Chaplin had arranged an interview for me with a martial arts magazine. He picked me up at the hotel and drove me to the interview. On the way he asked me, "What do you call your style?" I answered that I had practiced many styles and systems but I didn't have a name for my own. Chaplin replied, "If the interviewer asks, why don't you tell him that it is called 'Wei Kuen Do?'" I asked, "What does that mean?" He explained that "Wei" means "assimilation," as in the digestion of food in the stomach; "Kuen" means "fist;" and "Do" means "the Way." This is how the Way of the Integrated Fist was first conceived.

Forty-three years later Wei Kuen Do has grown into a system that is not confined by structure. It continues to grow and evolve, assimilating the characteristics of those who embrace it. Like water, the substance of Wei Kuen Do is integration and adaptability—"if you put water in a cup, it becomes the cup..." Unlike many martial arts systems that are fixed and rigidly structured, Wei Kuen Do has firmly planted roots, but branches that can take on the shape of the environment and adapt to the individual practitioner.

Members of the Wei Kuen Do family come from many styles and traditions. It is my conviction that whatever style they practice forms the foundation and direction of their martial journey, and Wei Kuen Do serves as the tool to integrate what is already there. Bruce Lee came from the Wing Chun tradition. No matter what he did with Jeet Kune Do, it retained shades of Wing Chun. I came from a Western Boxing tradition. No matter what I do with Wei Kuen Do, there will always be a major Boxing influence in my approach.

澢拳道

A good example of my art's Boxing roots is the Trap Boxing aspect of Wei Kuen Do. The trapping concept came from my exposure to Wing Chun through Bruce Lee and James Lee. But my mind-set remained grounded in Boxing. When I trained in Serrada Escrima with Angel Cabales in the 1970s I tried to follow his directions when it came to free sparring, but sometimes my Boxing techniques automatically kicked in. I often ended up hitting Angel on the head with the sticks!

Whatever direction we choose to go in our development; whatever theories and concepts we practice, the ultimate goal is to be efficient in free-fighting. In my conversations with Bruce during the early 1970s, he came up with three steps to developing spontaneous responses to free-fighting attacks: Developing the Tools, Refining the Tools and Dissolving the Tools. He used the analogy of a voice and an echo. After his death I started to think of it terms of compliance and non-compliance: It is easy to make your techniques work when your partner is compliant. In the arena of competition or on the street, however, you must face non-compliance. The attacker is trying to destroy you. In realizing this, I came up with a fourth step: Expressing the Tools.

At the highest level, free-fighting involves expressing yourself in the context of non-compliant combat. You may use kicks, punches or grappling, but you must <u>express</u>, and not merely repeat from memory. The ultimate goal of Wei Kuen Do is to teach the practitioner how to express himself within the context of the martial arts. This manual—assembled by a senior Wei Kuen Do instructor—is the foundation upon which this art is built. When practiced properly and sincerely, nothing can overpower it.

—Leo T. Fong

YOUR WEI KUEN DO JOURNEY

♦   ♦

My Wei Kuen Do journey began...

滙拳道

WEI KUEN DO

滙拳道

WEI KUEN DO

滙拳道

APPENDIX A—THE WKD STRAIGHT

The basic techniques and principles of Wei Kuen Do can be easily remembered by using the mnemonic of a "straight":

- **Seven** defenses: (1) the shoulder roll; (2) the regular parry; (3) the "punishing" parry; (4) the "clearing" parry; (5) the leg parry; (6) the deflection; and (7) the cross-redirection.

- **Six** basic hand techniques: (1) the punch (jab or straight); (2) the hook; (3) the uppercut; (4) the hammerfist; (5) the axefist; and (6) the backfist.

- **Five** basic principles: (1) the falling step; (2) the power of the hook; (3) the power of combinations; (4) "milling" on the retreat; and (5) the V-step.

- **Four** basic leg techniques: (1) the front kick; (2) the side kick; (3) the "hook<u>ing</u>" kick (like a low roundhouse); and (4) the "sweep<u>ing</u>" kick (like stepover kick).

- **Three** Modern Escrima strikes that differ from the Modern Arnis 12: (1) left wrist/rib; (2) right wrist/rib; and (3) rising (usually to the groin).

APPENDIX B—THE TEN WKD PRINCIPLES

滙拳道

最好的在你心中
The ultimate is within you

精神先於思想。思想先於身體
Spirit before mind, mind before body

好的練習將使響應自動進行
Proper practice makes for reflexive response

等待合適的時機進攻
Wait for the right moment to attack

不要透露你的攻擊
Attack without telegraphing

有控制地捍衛
Defend with control

聽你的敵人
Listen to what your opponent is "saying"

順其自然
Don't try to drive the situation; surf it!

贏得或學習
Don't win or lose—win or learn

知道什麼時候走開
Know when to walk away from the "boat" that carried you

滙拳道

ABOUT THE AUTHORS

As with any list of acknowledgements, there is a fair chance that the editors will inadvertently neglect to mention kind and valuable contributions from one source or another. In an effort to avoid any such omission, it should be recognized that this work in its entirety is the product of the collaborative efforts of many of Grandmaster Leo Fong's friends, family, students and colleagues, and that each person whose name appears in this book has provided significant support to this special project. It is for this reason that authorship is collectively attributed to Leo's friends and students. Having said that, it is appropriate to provide specific recognition for several individuals without whose assistance this work could not have been completed at all. Accordingly, the editors wish to thank:

☯ **Ross Dworkin**: For his valuable input and vital assistance in obtaining many of the illustrations for this work.

☯ **Grandmaster Adam James:** For patiently answering countless technical question and tirelessly filling in conceptual gaps all along the way.

☯ **Grandmaster Shane Lear:** For his kind support, particularly with respect to the Trapping Combinations section of this work.

☯ **Grandmaster Dr. Thomas Nardi:** For providing a wealth of historical information and an abundance of encouragement at the outset and beyond.

☯ **Grandmaster Dusty Seale:** For his generous assistance, especially with the Acronym, Analogy, Alliteration section of the book.

☯ **Grandmaster Dr. Charles Terry:** For decades of mentoring, encouragement and comradeship along the path on which this work is the most recent milestone.

WEI KUEN DO

www.ingramcontent.com/pod-product-compliance
Lightning Source LLC
Chambersburg PA
CBHW050634160426
43194CB00010B/1672